CONSTITUTIONAL AND ADMINISTRATIVE LAW

Revision WorkBook

Editors: R. Hughes LLB, CQSW and S. Migdal Barrister

GW00503878

HLT Publications

HLT PUBLICATIONS
200 Greyhound Road, London W14 9RY

© The HLT Group Ltd 1990

ISBN 1 85352 750 5

British Library Cataloguing-in-Publication.

A CIP Catalogue record for this book is available from the
British Library.

Printed and bound in Great Britain.

CONTENTS

ACKNOWLEDGEMENT

Some questions used are taken or adapted from past University of London LLB (External) Degree examination papers and our thanks are extended to the University of London for their kind permission to use and publish the questions.

Caveat

The LLB answers given are not approved or sanctioned by the University of London and are entirely our responsibility.

They are not intended as 'Model Answers', but rather as Suggested Solutions.

The answers have two fundamental purposes, namely:

a) To provide a detailed example of a suggested solution to an examination question, and

b) To assist students with their research into the subject and to further their understanding and appreciation of the subject of Law.

INTRODUCTION

This Revision WorkBook is aimed to be of help to those studying constitutional and administrative law. Its coverage is not restricted to any one syllabus but embraces all the core topics which can be found in university and polytechnic examinations.

Students will hopefully find it useful not only at examination time but also as a helpful summary of and introduction to the subject when studying it for the first time.

The WorkBook has been designed specifically to address common problems suffered by students when studying any legal subject. All examination based courses consist of four main processes, all of which may cause problems for some students. The WorkBook can be of help with each of these processes.

a) *Acquisition of knowledge*

This is achieved by individual work - attending lectures and reading the relevant textbooks and source materials such as cases and articles. The WorkBook is not intended to be a textbook and is in no way a substitute for one. However, the 'key points' and 'recent cases and statutes' sections will help students to direct their study to the important areas within each topic.

b) *Understanding*

Whilst difficulties in understanding a topic or particular point are best solved by a teacher's explanation. The WorkBook offers a summary of the essential points together with cases. This is the key to understanding for many students.

c) *Learning*

The process of learning is also a highly individual one. As a rule, however, students find it much easier to learn within a clear structure. The WorkBook will be an aid to those who find learning a problem.

d) *Applying the knowledge to the question*

This is, perhaps, the most common problem of all. The WorkBook includes examination questions and answers covering many possible question variations within each topic. All such 'model answers' are of a length which a student could reasonably be expected to produce under the time restraints of an examination.

HOW TO STUDY CONSTITUTIONAL AND ADMINISTRATIVE LAW

Constitutional and administrative law is a vast subject covering a variety of topics ranging from the structure and organisation of government to civil liberties. Examiners must be selective be in the areas they choose to examine and students should pay regard to their particular syllabus and the emphasis placed on each topic. By and large however the subject divides into three areas - the characteristics of the British Constitution, judicial review of administrative action and civil liberties.

The first part of any syllabus - usually the characteristics of the British Constitution - demands a background knowledge of British history and politics. This can cause problems for students who do not have any interest or knowledge of this area and overseas students in particular can experience difficulty here. To place the subject in its proper context requires some background reading - Maitland's *A Constitutional History of England* is authoritative - and knowledge gleaned from keeping abreast of current affairs is vital. In addition there are several good introductory works which help students. In terms of the examination this area can unsettle students simply because there is an absence of legal authority for the points they make. The questions are often discursive demanding the discussion of an issue and the presentation of a point of view. A well-read student who can present the salient points with authority will achieve good marks - the student who 'waffles' will not. Examples are important eg answer to a question on conventions demands an explanation of the part played by convention in our constitution backed by examples of conventions in operation.

The next part of a syllabus is judicial review of administrative action. This is an important area usually forming a significant part of the course. Administrative law within a constitutional law syllabus can only be dealt with in outline but students must know the procedure for seeking judicial review, the public/private law divide, the doctrine of ultra vires and the requirements of natural justice. There has been what has been described an an 'explosion' of case law in this area of law but reliance must be placed on the major cases cited in the text books which exemplify the basic points. Examination questions are often problem based and evidently the skills in answering them are comparable to other case law subjects. Students should be sure to advise who they are asked to in the question and support their answer within authority from case law.

Finally the syllabus will deal with civil liberties. Again this is an extensive area and examiners are often selective. Police powers may appear in some syllabuses, citizenship and immigration in others. It is important to appreciate that what liberties are enjoyed in the United Kingdom are residual and the part played by the European Convention on Human Rights must be understood. The subject matter is topical, statute and case law are important. Questions can be either essay or problem - for example an essay on a Bill of Rights for the United Kingdom is frequently examined and demands that students present the argument both for and against the adoption in the United Kingdom of a written Bill of Rights. Problem questions, for example on public order or police powers, require students to apply the relevant statute and case law to the facts given, remembering again to take care to advise the person they have been asked to.

In essence constitutional and administrative law, like all legal subjects, requires students to present arguments in a precise, reasoned and authoritative manner.

REVISION AND EXAMINATION TECHNIQUE

(A)   REVISION TECHNIQUE

Planning a revision timetable

In planning your revision timetable make sure you don't finish the syllabus too early. You should avoid leaving revision so late that you have to 'cram' - but constant revision of the same topic leads to stagnation.

Plan ahead, however, and try to make your plans increasingly detailed as you approach the examination date.

Allocate enough time for each topic to be studied. But note that it is better to devise a realistic timetable, to which you have a reasonable chance of keeping, rather than a wildly optimistic schedule which you will probably abandon at the first opportunity!

The syllabus and its topics

One of your first tasks when you began your course was to ensure that you thoroughly understood your **syllabus**. Check now to see if you can write down the **topics** it comprises from memory. You will see that the chapters of this WorkBook are each devoted to a topic. This will help you decide which are the key chapters relative to your revision programme. Though you should allow some time for glancing through the other chapters.

The topic and its key points

Again working from memory, analyse what you consider to be the key points of any topic that you have selected for particular revision. Seeing what you can recall, unaided, will help you to understand and firmly memorise the concepts involved.

Using the WorkBook

Relevant questions are provided for each topic in this book. Naturally, as typical examples of examination questions, they do not normally relate to one topic only. But the questions in each chapter *will* relate to the subject matter of the chapter to a degree. You can choose your method of consulting the questions and solutions, but here are some suggestions (strategies 1-3). Each of them pre-supposes that you have read through the author's notes on key points and question analysis, and any other preliminary matter, at the beginning of the chapter. Once again, you now need to practise working from *memory*, for that is the challenge you are preparing yourself for. As a rule of procedure constantly test yourself once revision starts, both orally and in writing.

Strategy 1

Strategy 1 is planned for the purpose of *quick revision*. First read your chosen question carefully and then jot down in abbreviated notes what you consider to be the main points at issue. Similarly, note the cases and statutes that occur to you as being relevant for citation purposes. Allow yourself sufficient time to cover what you feel to be relevant. Then study the author's *skeleton solution* and skim-read the *suggested solution* to see how they compare with your notes. When comparing consider carefully what the author has included (and concluded) and see whether that agrees with what you have written. Consider the points of variation also. Have you recognised the key issues? How relevant have you been? It is possible, of course, that you have referred to a recent case that *is* relevant, but which had not been reported when the WorkBook was prepared.

Strategy 2

Strategy 2 requires a nucleus of *three hours* in which to practise writing a set of examination answers in a limited time-span.

Select a number of questions (as many as are normally set in your subject in the examination you are studying for), each from a different chapter in the WorkBook, without consulting the solutions. Find a place to write where you will not be disturbed and try to arrange not to be interrupted for three hours. Write your solutions in the time allowed, noting any time needed to make up if you *are* interrupted.

After a rest, compare your answers with the *suggested solutions* in the WorkBook. There will be considerable variation in style, of course, but the bare facts should not be too dissimilar. Evaluate your answer critically. Be 'searching', but develop a positive approach to deciding how you would tackle each question on another occasion.

Strategy 3

You are unlikely to be able to do more than one three hour examination, but occasionally set yourself a single question. Vary the 'time allowed' by imagining it to be one of the questions that you must answer in three hours and allow yourself a limited preparation and writing time. Try one question that you feel to be difficult and an easier question on another occasion, for example.

Mis-use of suggested solutions

Don't try to learn by rote. In particular, don't try to reproduce the *suggested solutions* by heart. Learn to express the basic concepts in your own words.

Keeping up-to-date

Keep up-to-date. While examiners do not require familiarity with changes in the law during the three months prior to the examination, it obviously creates a good impression if you can show you are acquainted with any recent changes. Make a habit of looking through one of the leading journals - *Modern Law Review, Law Quarterly Review* or the *New Law Journal*, for example - and cumulative indices to law reports, such as the *All England Law Reports* or *Weekly Law Reports*, or indeed the daily law reports in *The Times*. Specialist journal(s) for the subject eg *Public Law* are also helpful sources.

(B)   EXAMINATION SKILLS

Examiners are human too!

The process of answering an examination question involves a *communication* between you and the person who set it. If you were speaking face to face with the person, you would choose your verbal points and arguments carefully in your reply. When writing, it is all too easy to forget *the human being who is awaiting the reply* and simply write out what one knows in the area of the subject! Bear in mind it is a person whose question you are responding to, throughout your essay. This will help you to avoid being irrelevant or long-winded.

The essay question

Candidates are sometimes tempted to choose to answer essay questions because they 'seem' easier. But the examiner is looking for thoughtful work and will not give good marks for superficial answers.

The essay-type of question may be either purely factual, in asking you to *explain the meaning* of a certain doctrine or principle, or it may ask you to *discuss* a certain proposition, usually derived from a quotation. In either case, the approach to the answer is the same. A clear programme must be devised to give the examiner the meaning or significance of the doctrine, principle or proposition and its origin in common law, equity or statute, and cases which illustrate its application to the branch of law concerned.

The problem question

The problem-type question requires a different approach. You may well be asked to advise a client or merely discuss the problems raised in the question. In either case, the most important factor is to take great care in reading the question. By its nature, the question will be longer than the essay-type question and you will have a number of facts to digest. Time spent in analysing the question may well save time later, when you are endeavouring to impress on the examiner the considerable extent of your basic legal knowledge. The quantity of knowledge is itself a trap and you must always keep within the boundaries of the question in hand. It is very tempting to show the examiner the extent of your knowledge of your subject, but if this is outside the question, it is time lost and no marks earned. It it inevitable that some areas which you have studied and revised will not be the subject of questions, but under no circumstances attempt to adapt a question to a stronger area of knowledge at the expense of relevance.

When you are satisfied that you have grasped the full significance of the problem-type question, set out the fundamental principles involved. You may well be asked to advise one party, but there is no reason why you should not introduce your answer by:

> 'I would advise A on the following matters ...'

and then continue the answer in a normal impersonal form. This is a much better technique than answering the question as an imaginary conversation.

You will then go on to identify the fundamental problem, or problems posed by the question. This should be followed by a consideration of the law which is relevant to the problem. The source of the law, together with the cases which will be of assistance in solving the problem, must then be considered in detail.

Very good problem questions are quite likely to have alternative answers, and in advising A you should be aware that alternative arguments may be available. Each stage of your answer, in this case, will be based on the argument or arguments considered in the previous stage, forming a conditional sequence.

If, however, you only identify one fundamental problem, do not waste time worrying that you cannot think of an alternative - there may very well be only that one answer.

The examiner will then wish to see how you use your legal knowledge to formulate a case and how you apply that formula to the problem which is the subject of the question. It is this positive approach which can make answering a problem question a high mark earner for the student who has fully understood the question and clearly argued his case on the established law.

Examination checklist

1   Read the instructions at the head of the examination carefully. While last-minute changes are unlikely - such as the introduction of a *compulsory question* or *an increase in the number of questions asked* - it has been known to happen.

2   Read the questions carefully. Analyse problem questions - work out what the examiner wants.

3   Plan your answer *before* you start to write. You can divide your time as follows:

(a)   working out the question (5 per cent of time)

(b)   working out how to answer the question (5 to 10 per cent of time)

(c)   writing your answer

Do not overlook (a) and (b)

4   Check that you understand the rubric *before* you start to write. Do not 'discuss', for example, if you are specifically asked to 'compare and contrast'.

5   Answer the correct number of questions. If you fail to answer one out of four questions set you lose 25 per cent of your marks!

Style and structure

Try to be clear and concise. Basically this amounts to using paragraphs to denote the sections of your essay, and writing simple, straightforward sentences as much as possible. The sentence you have just read has 22 words - when a sentence reaches 50 words it becomes difficult for a reader to follow.

Do not be inhibited by the word 'structure' (traditionally defined as giving an essay a beginning, a middle and an end). A good structure will be the natural consequence of setting out your arguments and the supporting evidence in a logical order. Set the scene briefly in your opening paragraph. Provide a clear conclusion in your final paragraph.

TABLE OF CASES

TABLE OF STATUTES

From the European Community

1   THE NATURE OF CONSTITUTIONAL LAW

1.1   Introduction

1.2   Key points

1.1   Introduction

Constitutions define political authority and the basis for the exercise of political authority. They regulate the relationships of the principle organs of government - legislature, executive and judiciary - to each other and define their function. A Constitution is essentially a framework of rules which make up the system whereby a state is governed.

In most modern states these rules are contained in a single document and usually include a Bill of Rights which guarantees to citizens of that state certain liberties. Such Constitutions are subject to judicial interpretation. The United Kingdom has no written Constitution and the sources are contained in statute, the common law and custom, usages and convention. Conventions play an important part in the United Kingdom but cannot be enforced in the courts.

1.2   Key points

a)   *Written and unwritten Constitutions*

The term 'written Constitution' is used in relation to those countries with a single document that contains the basic rules and to which reference can be made. By contrast with an 'unwritten Constitution' no such document exists and the rules have to be established from the ordinary laws of the land.

b)   *Flexible and rigid Constitutions*

Most countries with a written Constitution require some special procedure before constitutional changes can be effected - for example a referendum or a two thirds majority of the Houses of Parliament. Flexible Constitutions are so described because constitutional change can be achieved by the same procedure as changes in laws generally. This is the position in the United Kingdom.

c)   *Other classifications*

i)   A system of government which is accountable to the people is described as democratic government. Constitutions define the way in which a government is to be responsible and the way in which it is elected.

ii)   Federal states are those states in which regions enjoy autonomous law making power. Unitary states are those in which power is focused on central government. The United Kingdom has a unitary system of government in that Parliament is the supreme law making body, while the United States is a federal state.

1

iii)   The head of state can vary in form. It may be a monarch, a president or a chairman. The extent of their powers is defined by the Constitution so that, for example, while the President of the USA enjoys significant powers, the President of the Republic of Ireland enjoys a position analogous to our own Monarch - that is to say most of their executive powers are exercised by ministers.

d)   A Constitution is in a sense a higher form of law. It is the basis upon which all other laws derive their validity and force. However it remains valid only for as long as those subject to it accept its rules as binding. It can be argued that acceptance can be imposed as in a dictatorship.

Students need to appreciate the basic features of Constitutions to provide a reference point from which to analyse the British Constitution.

2 THE CHARACTERISTICS OF THE BRITISH CONSTITUTION

2.1 Introduction

2.2 Key points

2.3 Recent cases and statutes

2.4 Analysis of questions

2.5 Questions

2.1 Introduction

The British Constitution has evolved over centuries and the 'rules' of constitutional behaviour are not contained in any single document. A point of comparison can be made with the USA where following the American War of Independence a written document was prepared which established fundamental constitutional principles and safeguarded the rights of citizens.

Our constitution has evolved over a period of time and through the actual process of government 'rules' have emerged which relate to our constitutional order. It is these rules and their application that must be understood.

The Constitution of the United Kingdom applies throughout England, Wales, Scotland and Northern Ireland. There is one government for the UK - the Constitution is unitary and not federal - and again a point of comparison is the American Constitution where the states have certain original law making powers. Government is monarchical but the role of the monarch is largely symbolic and the exercise of powers is controlled by convention. Government is democratic in the sense that membership of the House of Commons is dependent on election and the government is accountable for the exercise of power although it is worth noting that government dominates the legislature.

2.2 Key points

a) *Sources of the Constitution*

Because we have an unwritten Constitution the sources are to be found in the general law ie statute and precedent and in practices that have become firmly established over time ie conventions.

i) Statute

There are many statutes which relate either to the system of government or to the rights of citizens. The problem of course is identifying all relevant legislation. Some examples are:

- The Bill of Rights 1689 which laid down the foundations of the modern Constitution.

3

- The Act of Settlement 1700 which provided for the succession to the throne.

- The Parliament Acts 1911 and 1949 which limited the powers of the House of Lords.

- The Police and Criminal Evidence Act 1984 which includes for example the rights of citizens on arrest or in police custody.

ii) Case law

Important decisions of the superior courts can have constitutional import and through the doctrine of binding precedent become an established constitutional principle. Some examples are:

- Remedies of the individual against the administration - the rules of natural justice and the doctrine of ultra vires.

- Prerogative power see *CCSU v Minister for the Civil Service* [1984] 3 All ER 935.

- The writ of Habeus Corpus.

iii) Conventions

Definition: Conventions are 'rules of the constitutional behaviour which are considered to be binding by and upon those who operate the Constitution but which are not enforced by the law courts ... nor by the presiding officers of the House of Parliament.'(Dicey) Some examples of conventions are:

- The monarchy
    - The Sovereign should act on the advice of her Ministers.
    - The Sovereign should ask the leader of the party with a majority in the House of Commons to form a government.
    - The Sovereign should dissolve Parliament at the request of the Prime Minister.
    - The Sovereign should not refuse the Royal Assent to Bills.

- The executive
    - Ministers are collectively and individually responsible to Parliament.
    - Ministers must be members of the House of Commons or House of Lords.
    - The government must resign if it loses the confidence of the Commons.

- Parliament
    - Public expenditure measures should originate in the House of Commons.

- The House of Lords ought ultimately defer to the will of the House of Commons.

- Judiciary

    - A judge's professional conduct should not be questioned in either House except on a motion for his dismissal.
    - A judge shall not be active in party politics.

The enforceability of conventions: The UK Constitution is described as flexible. Conventions allow changes in the Constitution to be achieved without formal change in the law. The question remains as to whether there are sanctions in the event of breach.

- Political sanctions

    The breach of some conventions would have far reaching consequences which could in some cases result in illegality ie the Royal Assent. Others would arouse great political controversy if not adhered to ie the resignation of the government on a vote of no confidence.

    Note that because conventions are not precisely formulated, political controversies sometimes occur about their scope.

- The courts

    Conventions are not enforceable in the courts because they are not rules of law: see *Madzimbamuto* v *Lardner-Burke* [1969] 1 AC 645. However the courts do recognise the existence of conventions: see *Attorney-General* v *Jonathan Cape* [1976] QB 752; *Liversidge* v *Anderson* [1942] AC 206.

b)   *The separation of powers*

The three basic and essential organs of state are legislative, executive and judicial. With a view to avoiding the potential for an autocratic and tyrannical form of government it has been considered theoretically desirable for the functions to be kept separate. In the late seventeenth century the French jurist Montesquieu developed the doctrine of the separation of powers which argues the need for checks and balances to exist between the three. It is a useful concept for analysing the nature of our parliamentary democracy.

i)   Legislature and executive

There is a significant overlap. Ministers head departments of state. The government initiates legislation and has the controlling voice in Parliament. Ministers and Local Authorities have a limited law making function through delegated legislation.

ii)   Executive and judiciary

The Lord Chancellor heads the judiciary, presides in the House of Lords and has a seat in Cabinet. Judges are appointed by the Lord Chancellor or by the Queen on the advice of the Lord Chancellor.

The judiciary control the executive authorities from exceeding their powers: see *Associated Provincial Picture Houses Ltd* v *Wednesbury Corporation* [1948] 1 KB 223.

iii) Judiciary and legislature

A degree of separation exists: House of Commons Disqualification Act 1975. Judges do, however, to a certain extent make law: see *Shaw* v *DPP* [1962] AC 220.

Within our Constitution Parliament is supreme and the courts cannot challenge an Act of Parliament. In many countries with written Constitutions the courts can challenge an act of the legislature as unconstitutional: see *Pickin* v *British Railways Board* [1974] AC 765.

c) *The rule of law*

At an abstract level the rule of law is simply stated. It is that law must conform to some minimum standards of justice, that the powers of government should be kept in check and that law and order should be maintained.

Dicey's propositions:

i) No man is punishable except for a distinct breach of the law and then only in the ordinary courts and in the manner prescribed by the law.

This is contrasted with arbitrary and discretionary powers. Governments in the twentieth century do enjoy wide discretionary powers although attempts are made to ensure accountability.

ii) No-one is above the law and everyone should be subject to the jurisdiction of the ordinary courts: *Entick* v *Carrington* (1765) 19 St Tr 1030.

iii) Principles of constitutional law are contained in judicial decisions which serve to ensure that individual liberties are protected. This is contrasted with the position in countries with a written Constitution where a single document - 'Bill of Rights' - seeks to establish the individual's rights.

Many question whether individual liberties are properly protected in our Constitution.

2.3   Recent cases and statutes

An up to date knowledge of recent political debate is important. For example the Local Government Finance Act 1988 was described in some debates as contrary to the rule of law as was the Prevention of Terrorism Act 1986 which allows the Home Secretary to authorise detention without access to a court for up to seven days.

Some point to recent developments in the style of Cabinet government as undermining the conventions that apply to that forum. This also has implications for the separation of powers.

The Canada Act 1982 involved the UK government considering the applicability of conventions in the request for patriation.

2.4   Analysis of questions

Questions on conventions are popular with examiners. Care must be taken to answer the question asked and not simply provide the examiner with a 'list'. The separation of powers and the rule of law may be examined in their own right but remember that both are concepts which can be used as a yardstick to evaluate other topics ie prime ministerial power or a Bill of Rights, both which come later in the syllabus.

2.5   Questions

QUESTION 1

Phrases like 'the separation of powers' and the 'rule of law' have no application to the British Constitution which rests solely on the principle of parliamentary sovereignty.

Discuss.

University of London LLB Examination
(for External Students) Constitutional Law June 1988 Q4

General comment

Not a difficult question, but an explanation of the doctrine of the separation of powers, and of the rule of law is required. The statement assumes that the British Constitution is based upon the doctrine of parliamentary sovereignty, and whilst this may well be true it is an assumption that needs to be considered.

Skeleton solution

Explain doctrine of separation of powers - provide examples of breach and observance - comment on importance. Similarly analyse the rule of law - consider Dicey's three propositions - example of each - conclusions on importance. Consider the theory of sovereignty and what it means in practical terms for the Constitution - give examples. Conclusion.

Suggested solution

Is the doctrine of the separation of powers irrelevant in the British Constitution? The doctrine is based on the principle that the powers of the legislature, judiciary, and executive should be in different hands, so as to provide for a system of checks and balances between each branch of government. Under the Constitution of the United States for example, the legislature, in the form of Congress, can veto the President's nominations for Supreme Court appointments. Similarly, the Supreme Court can invalidate legislation enacted by Congress, on the ground that it is 'unconstitutional'.

If one examines the British Constitution it is undoubtedly the case that one will find many examples of the doctrine being violated. Ministers, members of the executive, are allowed to sit as members of the legislative body, the House of Commons. Judges have a role in creating law, by virtue of their powers to 'discover' or develop the common law, a clear example of which is provided by *Shaw* v *DPP* (1962) ; arguably this involves the judiciary in usurping, or at least duplicating, the functions of the legislature.   Further many executive bodies such as tribunals and

7

commissioners exercise 'judicial' functions, by determining the rights of an applicant to some benefit or compensation.

To suggest, however, that the doctrine of the separation of powers is thus of 'no application' to the British Constitution is, it is submitted, to go too far. One of the main purposes of the House of Commons Disqualification Act 1975 was to simplify the law relating to the involvement of members of the executive in the legislature. As a result, the number of government ministers permitted to sit in the House of Commons is strictly limited at 95. Civil servants must resign their posts in order to stand for election to the House; police officers and members of the armed forces are also disqualified from membership of the House. The doctrine of the separation of powers is also reflected in the fact that a Member of Parliament, although unable to resign from office, can disqualify himself by taking an 'office of profit under the Crown', such as Stewardship of the Chiltern Hundreds.

If the doctrine is really of little significance to the British Constitution, it is difficult to explain the importance attached to judicial review. By means of an application for judicial review judges are able to call upon their common law jurisdiction to adjudicate upon the legality of action taken by administrative agencies, which includes members of the executive such as ministers; for a striking example of this see *Padfield* v *Minister of Agriculture* (1968).

It is not easy to determine the importance of the rule of law to the British Constitution until one has explained what is meant by the concept. If one adopts a Dicean approach the rule of law encompasses three notions, firstly the absolute predominance of regular law as opposed to the influence of arbitrary power, secondly equality of all subjects before the law, and thirdly that so-called constitutional law is simply the law of the land applied to the Constitution.

As to the first of these notions, Dicey rejected 'arbitrary' power as being contrary to the rule of law, but in the modern state legislation is frequently enacted granting to ministers powers to act as they think fit in a given situation. The existence of such subjectively worded powers does not mean, however, that ministers can become a law unto themselves. Again one comes back to the significant role played within the Constitution by judicial review. In *Padfield* v *Minister of Agriculture* (above), the House of Lords confirmed that the courts would not be inhibited from invalidating a minister's action simply because he purported to act within a broadly drafted power.

Equality of subjects before the law is perhaps less easy to establish in English law, if for no other reason than one party to litigation may be able to afford a more competent legal advisor than the other. Even if one takes the proposition to mean that no one is above the law and that the law applies equally to all, difficulties will still arise by virtue of the number of exceptions that can be cited.

Parliamentary privilege prevents MPs from being sued in respect of statements made in proceedings in Parliament, the immunities of foreign diplomats are well known, and judges enjoy various legal privileges as an incident of their holding office. Further, children under the age of ten are not subject to the criminal law. It is submitted, however, that these examples do not actually undermine the argument supporting the existence of the rule of law in the British Constitution, but in fact add strength to it, since they are all examples of exemptions granted and recognised by law. It is certain that they could all be abolished or amended by law.

The third aspect of Dicey's theory of the rule of law is the most questionable, and arguably the least relevant to the modern British Constitution. Dicey's view seems to reject the idea that there could be a body of law known as 'public law' as distinct from the private law governing individual rights and duties. That Dicey should reject such an idea is not surprising given his suspicion that it might involve public bodies being above the law, or at least enjoying legal privileges in comparison with the private individual. Today it has to be accepted that there is a branch of law, dealing with government and administration which lawyers for convenience term as 'public law' but it has not necessarily resulted in the type of abuse Dicey might have feared.

Turning to parliamentary sovereignty, it would be foolish indeed to undermine the importance of this doctrine to the British Constitution, since it is in many ways what marks it out as being different from many other constitutions. It does mean that the judiciary will refuse to invalidate legislation which has been enacted by Parliament, see *Pickin* v *British Railways Board* (1974). It also means that Parliament can enact legislation effectively nullifying a decision by the highest court, see *Burmah Oil Co* v *Lord Advocate* (1965) as followed by the War Damage Act 1965. Whether it is still as strong a constitutional force as it once was is, however, questionable. The contention that parliamentary sovereignty meant that no Parliament could bind its successors has always seemed dubious as regards legislation granting independence to former colonies and dominions. Parliament could vote to repeal the Canada Act 1982, but it is unlikely that the Canadians would give any effect to such a measure by recognising it. The debate over whether membership of the EEC has resulted in loss of sovereignty has been raging for nearly twenty years, but it is submitted that regardless of legal theory, there may well come a time when the United Kingdom is so firmly enmeshed in Europe that withdrawal ceases to be a practical option. What price parliamentary sovereignty then?

In conclusion it is submitted that if one had to cite the most significant aspect of the British Constitution it would be parliamentary sovereignty, but this would not be on the basis that concepts such as the rule of law and the doctrine of the separation of powers were either redundant or irrelevant.

QUESTION 2

To what extent, if any, do you agree with the statement that 'conventions constitute probably the most discussed and least definable source of the Constitution' (Norton).

University of London LLB Examination
(for External Students) Constitutional Law June 1987 Q1

General comment

A relatively difficult question. Unless you can deal with the specific point raised concerning the definition of conventions you should not attempt this question. The danger with such a question is that your answer becomes too general and there is the temptation to fill it out by simply producing a list of conventions.

Skeleton solution

* Introduction - what are conventions of the constitution?

* The difficulty of defining conventions. The lack of written form; their political nature; lack of legal form; effect of disagreement; absence of pre-existing usage; flexibility.

* Why conventions are discussed. Distinction between law and convention; why conventions are obeyed; the advantage of conventions over legal rules.

Suggested solution

A great many of the rules of the British Constitution, which are observed by the Sovereign, the Prime Minister, Ministers, Members of Parliament, the judiciary and civil servants, are not contained in Acts of Parliament or judicial decisions, but are to be found in those rules of conduct called constitutional conventions. These have been described as 'rules of constitutional behaviour which are considered to be binding by and upon those who operate the Constitution but which are not enforced by the law courts ... nor by the presiding officers in the Houses of Parliament': Marshall & Moodie, *Some Problems of the Constitution*, 5th ed 1971 pp22-23. These conventions of the Constitution are obeyed by those to whom they apply not because of the threat of any legal sanction in case of breach, but because of the political difficulties which may follow if they are not obeyed.

Some conventional rules are very well known and have great authority but many others have been developed on a very informal basis so as to avoid the sort of strictness one usually associates with changes in the law. This informality associated with conventions of the Constitution often means that, while some may be publicly recorded, others are not formulated in writing, having simply evolved as practice over a period of time. It is for this reason that at a given moment in time it may be impossible to ascertain whether practice on a certain matter has crystallised into a conventional rule. This, together with the fact that they operate in a political context, often means that disputes may arise about the existence and content of conventional rules. Whereas disputes about the existence and content of legal rules are settled by judicial decisions, no formal judicial mechanism exists to settle disputes concerning conventional rules.

Problems may arise therefore when attempting to identify conventional rules. By their definition conventions of the Constitution are forms of political behaviour based upon usage and regarded as obligatory, but at the same time lacking legal sanction. But when or how does such a non-binding usage become binding? One answer is of course that usage becomes binding because those to whom the usage applies consider that there is an obligation on their part to continue to behave in that way. But the dominant motive is not always apparent. Is the usage obeyed out of a sense of obligation or for some other reason? Also, what if there is substantial disagreement as to the existence or content of a convention. Political expediency or personal prejudice may result in divided interpretations of the obligation, if any, to be assumed. Certainly the opinions of politicians may differ as to the scope of the conventions they should observe. The fact that conventions may be created without any evidence of pre-existing usage also results in problems of identification.

Their non-legal nature also means that conventions are very flexible in the sense that they may lose their binding force or undergo a change in content without the need for any formal mechanism being followed. Conventions established by express agreement may be superseded or changed by agreement. Decisions taken by the Prime Minister or the Cabinet about the way Cabinet is to operate, for example, may be superseded by new decisions. Changes in circumstance may result in a convention losing its force, or indeed, the fact that a convention has been disregarded with impunity. Other conventions disappear with general acquiescence.

It is therefore probably true to say that conventions constitute the least definable source of the Constitution. They are also probably the most discussed source especially as regards their interrelationship with the legal rules of the Constitution. The differences between law and convention, the reasons why conventions are obeyed, whether or not conventions should be codified as law and the attitudes of the courts towards conventions are all matters which have occupied constitutional writers for many years and no doubt will continue to do so into the future.

QUESTION 3

'A written Constitution for the United Kingdom would preserve the best of the existing constitutional practices and would remove the major defects.'

Discuss.

University of London LLB Examination
(for External Students) Constitutional Law June 1986 Q2

General comment

A difficult question which should only be attempted as a last resort.

Skeleton solution

- Introduction: What is a Constitution?: The unwritten nature of the United Kingdom Constitution.

- The defects of our constitutional system: the absence of a higher form of law; the sovereignty of Parliament.

- The benefits of our constitutional system: the flexible nature of the Constitution; the process of evolution.

- Conclusion: adoption of a written Constitution need not result in rigidity, but even if desirable is change necessary?

Suggested solution

The Constitution of a state may be defined as the body of rules relating to the structure, functions and powers of the organs of state, their relationship to one

11

another, and to the private citizen. The word 'constitution' is also used to refer to a document having a special legal sanctity which sets out the framework and the principal functions of the organs of government within the state, and declares the principles by which those organs must operate. This document has usually been enacted by the legislature or adopted by some other constituent body, for example a Constituent Assembly. In this sense of the word, as de Tocqueville observed, the United Kingdom has no Constitution. There is no single document from which is derived the authority of the main organs of government, such as the Crown, the Cabinet, Parliament and the courts of law. No single document lays down the relationship of the primary organs of government one with another, or with the people.

Within the United Kingdom therefore there is no written Constitution which can serve as fundamental law. This can create certain difficulties. In most states the Constitution is a higher form of law in the sense that other laws must conform with it. The Constitution imposes limits on what may be done by ordinary legislation and the courts may declare certain legislative acts void. But in the United Kingdom, in the absence of a written Constitution to serve as the foundation of the legal system, the vacuum is filled by the legal doctrine of the legislative supremacy of Parliament. The result is that formal restraints upon the exercise of power which exist in other states do not exist in the United Kingdom. Parliament may make or unmake any law. There is no limit to its competence to legislate. No Parliament may bind its successors or be bound by its predecessors and the courts cannot question the validity of an Act of Parliament.

A major defect therefore of the United Kingdom Constitution is that the absence of any higher form of law makes it virtually impossible to ensure that the rights of minorities and individual citizens are protected against legislative infringement by Parliament. Moreover, the absence of a written Constitution means that there is no special procedure prescribed for legislation of constitutional importance. For example, before the Republic of Ireland could join the EEC, a constitutional amendment to the Irish Constitution had to be approved by a referendum of the people. In the United Kingdom, however, while the European Communities Act 1972 was debated at length in Parliament, the Act was passed by essentially the same procedure as would apply to any legislation of purely domestic concern. The absence of a written Constitution means that in practice the British Constitution depends far less on legal rules and safeguards and relies much more upon political and democratic principles. But can the politicians be trusted to observe these informal restraints on their power?

These problems could, it is argued, be overcome if the United Kingdom adopted a formal written Constitution which defined the scope, and set out the legal limitations on, the functions and powers of the organs of government. But it must be remembered that no written document alone can ensure the smooth working of a system of government. A written document has no greater force than that which persons in authority are willing to attribute to it. Also our present unwritten Constitution founded as it is partly on Acts of Parliament and judicial decisions, partly upon political practice, and partly upon detailed procedures established by the various organs of government for carrying their own tasks, provides a complex and comprehensive system of government which has served the United Kingdom well. In particular, as all law in the United Kingdom, including laws relating to the Constitution, may be enacted, repealed or amended by the Queen in Parliament using the same legislative procedure, our Constitution is highly flexible and can adapt to meet changes in social, moral and political circumstances. Indeed this facility for gradual evolution has been one of the major contributions to the political and social stability of the United Kingdom.

But the adoption of a written Constitution need not necessarily destroy this flexibility altogether. A written Constitution cannot contain all the detailed rules upon which government depends and accordingly a written Constitution usually evolves a wide variety of customary rules and practices which attune the operation of the Constitution to changing conditions. These customary rules and practices will usually be more easily changed than the Constitution itself and their constant evolution will reduce the need for formal amendment of the written Constitution. For example the rules for electing the legislature are usually found not in the written Constitution but in ordinary statutes enacted by the legislature within the limits laid down by the Constitution. Such statutes can when necessary be amended by the ordinary process of legislation whereas amendments to the Constitution may require a more elaborate process, such as a special majority in the legislature or approval by a referendum.

Therefore it may well be the case that a written Constitution for the United Kingdom would preserve the best of the existing constitutional practices and would remove the major defects. But, in spite of the defects, so long as our present constitutional system works so well, why change?

QUESTION 4

Argue the case for and against codification in a legal form of the conventions of the British Constitution.

University of London LLB Examination
(for External Students) Constitutional Law June 1985 Q2

General comment

This is a very straightforward question involving discussion of conventions of the Constitution, the differences between law and convention and the arguments for and against the codification of conventions in a legal form.

Students should remember to stick to the specific points raised in the question. Don't write everything you know about conventions and don't simply produce a list of conventions.

Skeleton solution

- Introduction - What are conventions; why are they obeyed?

- Distinction between law and convention. Dicey's views contrasted with those of Jennings.

- Why maintain a distinction between law and convention?

- The advantages of codification of conventions in legal form: clarification of the present vague and undefined rules of conventions; the provision of a clear legal definition of unconstitutional behaviour; certainty.

- The advantages of retaining conventions: helps to bring about constitutional change without formal change in the law; flexibility helps to keep the judiciary out of political controversy.

Suggested solution

A great many rules of the British Constitution, which are observed by the Sovereign, the Prime Minister, Ministers, Members of Parliament, the Judiciary and civil servants, are not contained in Acts of Parliament or judicial decisions, but are to be found in those rules of conduct called constitutional conventions. These have been described as 'rules of constitutional behaviour which are considered to be binding by and upon those who operate the Constitution but which are not enforced by the law courts ... nor by the presiding officers in the House of Parliament': Marshall & Moodie, *Some Problems of the Constitution*, 5th ed 1971 pp22-23. These conventions of the Constitution are obeyed by those to whom they apply not because of the threat of any legal sanction in case of breach, but because of the political difficulties which may follow if they are not obeyed: see Jennings, *The Law and the Constitution*, 5th ed 1959, p134.

Conventions therefore differ from laws in that unlike laws they are not enforced by the courts. According to Dicey (*The Law of the Constitution* 10th ed 1959), conventions are not 'laws in the true sense of the word, for if any or all of them were broken, no court would take notice of their violation'. Laws are rules enforced and recognised by the courts whereas conventions are 'a body not of laws but of constitutional or political ethics - the constitutional morality of the day, not enforced or recognised by the courts'. However, this approach is too simplistic. Conventions of the Constitution are sometimes recognised by the courts. For example in *Carltona Ltd* v *Commissioners of Works* (1943), the court recognised the convention of ministerial responsibility. Also some rules of strict law may be non-justicable. According to Jennings (op cit), the real distinction between law and convention lies in the fact that legal rules are either formally expressed, or illustrated by a decision of a court, whereas conventions arise out of practice. Law and convention are however closely interlocked. Conventions, it is said, 'provide the flesh which clothes the dry bones of the law; they make the legal constitution work; they keep it in touch with the growth of ideas'.

The question therefore arises, why maintain the distinctions between strict law and convention? Why not codify conventions of the Constitution in a legal form? In theory, all the conventional rules of the Constitution could be enacted in legal form by one or more Acts of Parliament. Indeed, this has been achieved under several Commonwealth Constitutions. Such a step would have distinct advantages. Codification would for example clarify certain constitutional rules which are at present vague and undefined. It is unsatisfactory that major rules of the Constitution remain indeterminate. For instance, under what circumstances may the Queen dismiss her Prime Minister? If the Queen were to dismiss or to refuse to dismiss the Prime Minister under certain circumstances this would undoubtedly provoke controversy, because of the uncertainty surrounding the Queen's power of dismissal. This controversy would be avoided if the circumstances in which the Queen can and must dismiss her Prime Minister were set out in legal form. Also, where the rules of the Constitution are in legal form, legislative or executive acts which conflict with the Constitution may be held to be unconstitutional and therefore illegal. In the United Kingdom the absence of any fully legal constitutional code means that 'unconstitutional' has no definition. It is not always easy to determine whether the boundary between constitutional and unconstitutional behaviour has been crossed.

However, while codification may have the advantage of clarifying particular rules the disadvantages of such a step are considerable. Conventions cover such a diverse area and they differ so much in character that they cannot logically be included within a single code. Even if such an attempt were made it would be impossible to stop the process by which formal rules are gradually modified by bon-legal rules from starting all over again.

Conventions also have several distinct advantages over legal rules in the context of constitutional law. Firstly they provide a means of bringing about constitutional change without the need for a formal change in the law. For example, many conventions concern the powers of the Sovereign. They allow the legal powers of the Queen to remain intact, thus lending dignity to the affairs of State, while at the same time allowing the democratically elected government to actually exercise those powers. It may also be difficult or even harmful to define some important constitutional conventions. Codification may bring certainty, but only at the expense of flexibility. Law is rigid and may be difficult to change. Conventions on the other hand allow the Constitution to evolve and keep up to date with changing circumstances without the need for formal enactment or repeal of law. Law must also be followed in every case. Conventions, being flexible and unenforceable by the courts allow discretion to be exercised and can be waived if the particular circumstances make this desirable. Most conventions also concern matters of a political nature. Their non-legal nature thus helps keep the judiciary and the courts out of politics and political controversy. Experience in the Commonwealth has illustrated the difficulty that can arise when the courts become involved in politically sensitive situations.

Therefore, so long as conventions are obeyed there is no need for legal codification. Nevertheless, if a particular convention is disregarded then it can, if necessary, be

15

formally enacted and given legal status. For example, in 1909 the House of Lords ignored the convention that they must defer to the will of the House of Commons. The result was the enactment of the Parliament Act 1911 defining the relationship between the two Houses on a statutory basis.

3 SOVEREIGNTY OF PARLIAMENT

3.1 Introduction

3.2 Key points

3.3 Recent cases and statutes

3.4 Analysis of questions

3.5 Questions

3.1 Introduction

It is important to understand in outline the means by which Parliament's legislative supremacy came to be established, and to understand the ways in which the British Constitution differs markedly from countries with a written Constitution. The British Constitution has evolved out of the long struggle between the Crown and Parliament, which culminated in Parliament exercising the powers previously enjoyed by the Crown.

Countries with a written Constitution place limits on the legislature and the courts can rule whether an act of the legislature is 'unconstitutional'. This is the case for example with the American Constitution.

The major issue on sovereignty is the question whether any Parliament can entrench legislation - that is to say limit in some way its future repeal - which could of course be of importance in the enactment of a Bill of Rights for the UK.

3.2 Key points

The phrase 'sovereignty of Parliament' is generally used to mean the absence of any legal restraint on the legislative powers of the United Kingdom Parliament. This absence of legal restraint has three aspects - see a) to c) following.

a)   *Parliament is legally competent to legislate on any subject matter*

    i)   The Act of Settlement 1700 and His Majesty's Declaration of Abdication Act 1936.

    ii)   *Burmah Oil Co* v *Lord Advocate* [1965] AC 75 and the War Damage Act 1965.

    iii) *Mortensen* v *Peters* (1906) 14 SLT 227.

    iv)   Parliament Acts 1911 and 1949.

    v)   Ireland Act 1949 s1(2).

b) *No Parliament can bind its successors or be bound by its predecessors*

'There is one and only one limit to Parliament's legal power: it cannot detract from its own continuing sovereignty'. (Dicey, *Law of the Constitution*.)

i) A later Parliament can expressly repeal an earlier statute.

ii) A later Parliament can impliedly repeal an earlier statute: *Vauxhall Estates* v *Liverpool Corp* [1932] 1 KB 733; *Ellen Street Estates Ltd* v *Minister of Health* [1934] 1 KB 590.

c) *Once Parliament has legislated no court or other person can pass judgment upon the validity of the legislation*

All the courts may do when faced with an Act of Parliament is apply it, subject to their limited powers of statutory interpretation. At common law a Bill becomes an Act of Parliament when it has been approved by the House of Commons and the House of Lords (unless passed under the provisions of the Parliament Acts), and has received the Royal Assent. The enforcement of these procedural rules is entirely a matter for the House concerned and the courts refuse to consider the question as to whether there have been any procedural defects in the passage of a Bill through Parliament: *Pickin* v *British Railways Board* [1974] AC 765.

d) *Limitations upon the exercise of parliamentary sovereignty*

Only Parliament can limit its own sovereignty and such limitations must have been enacted in the form of a statute. However, no Parliament can bind its successors. Therefore whatever limitations are imposed upon the sovereignty of Parliament by one statute may be repealed by a subsequent Act. However, in practice there are limitations upon the sovereignty of Parliament.

i) Limitation as to the scope and subject matter of Parliamentary legislation: Statute of Westminster 1931 s4.

ii) Limitation as to the manner and form which legislation must take: *Attorney-General for New South Wales* v *Trethowan* [1932] AC 526 - but note that this applied to a colonial legislature.

iii) Other practical limitations on the exercise of sovereignty

• The doctrine of the mandate

• Public opinion

• Political and economic constraints

European Communities Act 1972

Northern Ireland Act 1973 s1

iv) Convention: Canada Act 1982; *Manuel* v *Attorney-General* [1983] Ch 87.

3.3   Recent cases and statutes

Canada Act 1982

Manuel v *Attorney-General* [1983] Ch 87

The above serve to emphasise the point that the courts will follow a statute despite the existence of an established convention.

3.4   Analysis of questions

Questions can be either essay or problem. Problem questions tend to focus on the issue as to whether or not Acts of Parliament can be entrenched against future repeal. Essay questions are more wide ranging and may examine the student's knowledge of the relationship between parliamentary sovereignty and conventions of the Constitution.

An example of each follows. Note that the problem question also demands a knowledge of the EC. (See chapter 4: *Sovereignty of Parliament and the EC.*)

3.5   Questions

QUESTION 1

In July 1984 Parliament based the Puffins Act: s1 provides that it shall be a criminal offence to kill a puffin; s2 provides that no Bill to repeal the Puffins Act shall be laid before Parliament unless the consent of the Birds Council has previously been obtained.

In 1985 a Bill repealing the Puffins Act is laid before Parliament, without the consent of the Birds Council having been previously obtained, and this is subsequently enacted as the Puffins Repeal Act 1985.

Advise the Birds Council whether they can challenge the 1985 Act and still bring a prosecution against Mr Toad who killed a puffin in 1986.

How, if at all, would your advice differ if the European Commission had made a Regulation in October 1984 providing that puffins were vermin and that a cash premium would be paid in respect of each puffin killed?

University of London LLB Examination
(for External Students) Constitutional Law June 1986 Q3

General comment

A relatively simple question on the sovereignty of Parliament and the effects of membership of the European Communities. As regards the first part of the question, after stating the content of the doctrine of parliamentary supremacy, students should argue as best they can the likely effect of the Puffins Repeal Act. There is no answer; just state the likely alternatives. The second part of the question is more straightforward as the supremacy of Community law over national rules is now firmly established in situations such as the one in the problem.

Skeleton solution

* Introduction: the content of the doctrine of parliamentary sovereignty.

* The Puffins Repeal Act 1985: the application of the doctrine of parliamentary sovereignty to the Act; the effects of s2 of the Act on the traditional doctrine.

* The European Communities Act 1972 s2(4); the supremacy of Community law over national laws.

Suggested solution

Under the doctrine of the sovereignty of Parliament there exists no legal limitation upon the legislative competence of the United Kingdom Parliament. This absence of legal restraint has three aspects: Parliament is legally competent to legislate upon any subject matter, no Parliament can bind its successors or be bound by its predecessors, and, once Parliament has legislated, no court or other person can pass judgment upon the validity of the legislation.

This rule that Parliament may not bind its successors (and that no Parliament is bound by Acts of its predecessors) is often cited both as a limitation upon legislative supremacy and as an example of it. As Dicey says, 'The logical reason why Parliament has failed in its endeavours to enact unchangeable enactments is that a sovereign power cannot, while retaining its sovereign character, restrict its own powers by any parliamentary enactment' (*The Law of the Constitution*, 10th edition, 1959, p68). It is inherent in the nature of a legislature that it should continue to be free to make new laws and, within the United Kingdom legal system therefore, all statutes that have been enacted by the Queen in Parliament remain in force until they are repealed or amended. An Act can be repealed either expressly or impliedly (see: *Ellen Street Estates* v *Minister of Health* (1934)). In the latter case if Parliament passes an Act which is contrary to a previous statute (or certain provisions of the earlier statute) the earlier statute (or those particular provisions) are held to have been repealed.

The doctrine therefore consists, in essence, of a rule which governs the legal relationship between the courts and the legislature, namely that the courts are under a duty to apply the legislation made by Parliament and may not hold an Act of Parliament to be invalid or unconstitutional.

Regarding the problem for consideration, in July 1984 Parliament passed the Puffins Act: s1 provides that it shall be a criminal offence to kill a puffin; s2 provides that no Bill to repeal the Puffins Act shall be laid before Parliament unless the consent of the Birds Council has previously been obtained. In 1985 a Bill repealing the Puffins Act is laid before Parliament, without the consent of the Birds Council having been previously obtained, and this is subsequently enacted as the Puffins Repeal Act 1985.

In order for the Birds Council to challenge the Puffins Repeal Act 1985 and prosecute Mr Toad, the Council will have to satisfy the courts that the Act is invalid due to the failure to comply with the consultation provisions of the 1984 Act. Normally of course, under the doctrine of parliamentary supremacy, there will be no problem. The courts will consider the 1985 Act to have expressly repealed the 1984 Act. But in the present case, what is the effect of s2? The principle that the Parliament which passed the 1984 Act cannot bind the Parliament which purports to enact the 1985 Repeal Act may mean simply that, notwithstanding s2, the repeal is valid and the courts will be bound to give effect to the express wishes of the legislature. However it can also be argued that s2 creates a provision as to the manner by which repeal of the 1984 Act must be achieved and that this will be binding upon future Parliaments until s2 itself is expressly repealed. Therefore any attempt to repeal the whole Act without first removing s2 will be invalid. Of course it may also be argued that by expressly repealing the whole of the 1984 Act Parliament is in any case impliedly repealing the consultation provisions of s2.

The situation concerning the effect of the purported repeal is therefore somewhat uncertain. No uncertainty would exist, however, had the European Commission made a Regulation in October 1984 providing that puffins were vermin and that a cash premium would be paid in respect of each puffin killed. Section 2(4) of the European Communities Act 1972 provides in effect that United Kingdom Acts of Parliament shall be construed and have effect subject to directly applicable Community law. Under Article 189 of the Treaty of Rome, Regulations have direct applicability and are binding in all member states without requiring implementation or adoption by national law. Therefore any Regulation made by the European Commission in October 1984 would have supremacy over national laws and take effect notwithstanding the conflict with the then already existing Puffins Act 1984. In this respect it is both clear from the Treaty and from statements made by the European Court of Justice (see: *Costa* v *ENEL* (1964)) that Community law should prevail over national law in all circumstances and therefore any United Kingdom constitutional law doctrine of the legislative supremacy of Parliament is irrelevant.

Of course, the approach taken by the European Court of Justice indicated above runs completely contrary to the traditional doctrine of the sovereignty of Parliament. This has resulted in controversy, with some arguing that, while the doctrine of implied repeal has been abandoned so far as Community law is concerned, the doctrine of express repeal of earlier law, including Community law, is nevertheless retained. However it is yet to be seen how the United Kingdom courts would act if faced by a United Kingdom Act of Parliament expressing an intention of Parliament to legislature contrary to Community law. Such a situation is, perhaps, unlikely to arise since it would amount to a blatant repudiation by the United Kingdom of its international obligations under the European Community Treaties. But, in the absence of such express repeal of Community law by our Parliament, it is clear that as in *Macarthy's Ltd* v *Smith* (1979), where a conflict does exist between United Kingdom legislation and Community law, the latter will prevail and accordingly, not withstanding the Puffins Act 1984 and its provisions, the Community Regulation of October 1984 will bind our courts.

QUESTION 2

Section 1 of the Northern Ireland Act 1973 reads:

' ... it is hereby affirmed that in no event will Northern Ireland ... cease to be part of ... the United Kingdom without the consent of the majority of the people of Northern Ireland voting in a poll held for the purposes of this section ...'

Is this a law or a convention or both? Is it a restriction on parliamentary sovereignty?

University of London LLB Examination
(for External Students) Constitutional Law June 1983 Q2

General comment

Be careful only to answer the question and not to digress into any sort of political discussion - it might be interesting but it is irrelevant for examination purposes. The question requires definitions and discussions of basic constitutional ideas - conventions and parliamentary sovereignty. It can be answered either under two separate headings or by amalgamating your answer into a continuous essay - but keeping both parts distinct.

Skeleton solution

• Relationship between law and convention.

• The courts and conventions.

• Soveriegnty of Parliament - doctrine of implied repeal.

• Political consequences. Statute of Westminster, European Communities Act 1972.

Suggested solution

In a number of constitutional contexts the distinction between law and convention is blurred. Dicey was quite clear that conventions were not 'laws' in the strict sense for if any were broken no court would 'recognise' them. Laws he felt were simply rules enforced or recognised by the court. But this is really over simplifying the nature of a convention for courts do take notice of conventions and use them as aids to interpretation. Constitutional conventions do influence judicial decisions. They may be compared to a preamble in an Act of Parliament.

Section 1 of the Northern Ireland Act is a curious case. It reads like the affirmation of a constitutional convention. It replaces s1(2) of the Ireland Act 1949 which stated the same thing but with a reference to the Parliament of Northern Ireland. As a constitutional convention it is binding on the United Kingdom Parliament but by placing it within the statute it might suggest it was a law. Generally matters within a statute are law and enforced and recognised by courts. Because it is within the statute it cannot be challenged in the courts as being void or unconstitutional. Statutes are the prime source of law and it would be a bold argument to suggest that s1 was not a law. If the government decided to ignore s1, without passing a statute, then a declaration could be sought to state that the government was acting unlawfully.

The extent of the Crown's prerogative powers can be determined by the courts and it can be impliedly fettered by a previous statute - following *Laker Airways Ltd* v *Dept of Trade* (1977). However, this control of the Crown prerogative is a recent innovation and is as yet untested in the House of Lords. The only remedy that could be obtained is a declaration which in practice would change the government decision but in strict legal theory it could be ignored.

Section 1 is a good example of the close relationship between law and convention. It is a law and might also be a convention. While it remains on the statute book it will be obeyed predominantly for political reasons and not through fear of litigation.

Is it a restriction on parliamentary sovereignty?

Parliamentary sovereignty is shorthand for the principle that Parliament is competent to make or unmake any law whatsoever on any matter whatsoever and that no court can question the validity of an Act of Parliament. Section 1 purports to bind future Parliaments and thus would seem to run contrary to the principle.

There is no method in law by which sections of statutes can be entrenched, and in strict legal terms Parliament could now pass an Act to grant independence to Northern Ireland or to cede it to Eire and thereby impliedly repeal s1. In his judgment in *Ellen Street Estates* v *Minister of Health* (1934) Maugham LJ stated 'The legislature cannot, according to our Constitution bind itself as to the form of subsequent legislation'. In reality it is unlikely that Northern Ireland would cease to be part of the United Kingdom without a referendum - the politics of the situation would demand it and it might be seen as political suicide to determine otherwise. Strictly s1 cannot be seen as a restriction on sovereignty.

Historically the formal giving away of parliamentary sovereignty by granting independence to a nation has followed the de facto independence of the country in question. This actual state of independence has not been reached and may never be reached in Northern Ireland.

4   SOVEREIGNTY OF PARLIAMENT AND THE EC

4.1 Introduction

4.2 Key points

4.3 Recent cases and statutes

4.4 Analysis of questions

4.5 Question

4.1   Introduction

a)   The political integration of European countries has been a post-war objective within Europe. In 1957 Belgium, France, West Germany, Italy, Luxembourg and the Netherlands signed the Treaty of Rome establishing the European Economic Community. In 1973 Denmark, Ireland and the United Kingdom became members.

b)   The United Kingdom became a member by virtue of the Treaty of Accession 1972. It was necessary for Parliament to pass legislation incorporating the provisions into domestic law. This was achieved by the European Communities Act 1972.

c)   Political and legal integration has proceeded since then. The political and legal issues which are at issue are:

   i)   The extent to which our Parliament is obliged to pass legislation which is consistent with the will of the community - a negation of sovereignty?

   ii)   The position of our courts where Community law and UK law conflict.

d)   Following the Single European Act 1986 the process of integration has continued apace. The removal of all trade barriers is an objective by 1992. These factors together with decisions of the European Court of Justice re-affirming the supremacy of Community law over national legislation is causing political controversy.

4.2   Key points

a)   *The sources of Community law*

   i)   The Treaties - member states must give effect to obligations arising under the Treaties.

   ii)   Acts of the Community Institutions - member states must take notice of acts of the Council and the Commission: Article 189. These are issued as directives or regulations.

24

iii) Decisions of the European Court

- Actions brought against member states.

- Rulings on the interpretation of 'Community law' referred by national courts: Article 177. See *Bulmer (HP) v J Bollinger SA* [1974] Ch 401.

b) *Direct applicability*

Section 2(1) of the European Communities Act 1972 provides:

'All such rights, powers, liabilities, obligations and restrictions from time to time created or arising by or under the Treaties, and all such remedies and procedures from time to time provided for by or under the Treaties, as in accordance with the Treaties are without further enactment to be given legal effect or used in the United Kingdom shall be recognised and available in law, and be enforced, allowed and followed accordingly; and the expression 'enforceable Community right' and similar expressions shall be read as referring to one to which this subsection applies.'

The effect of this subsection is that all the provisions of Community law which are, in accordance with Community law, intended to take direct effect in the United Kingdom are given the force of law. This applies to Community law made both before and after the coming into force of the Act.

c) *The supremacy of Community law over national rules*

Section 2(4) of the European Communities Act provides:

'The provision that may be made under subsection (2) above includes, subject to Schedule 2 of this Act, any such provision (of any such extent) as may be made by Act of Parliament, and any enactment passed or to be passed, other than one contained in this part of this Act, shall be construed and have effect subject to the forgoing provisions of this section.'

The 'forgoing provisions' include s2(1) which states that directly applicable Community law shall have effect in the United Kingdom. Therefore s2(4) seems to amount to a statement that United Kingdom Acts of Parliament 'shall be construed and have effect subject to' directly applicable Community law.

The primacy of Community law over UK law can be seen in decisions of the European Court of Justice: *Costa v ENEL* [1964] ECR 585.

d) *Community law and the UK*

European law will be followed in preference to inconsistent pre-1972 Statutes: *Conegate v HM Customs and Excise* [1987] 2 WLR 39.

It is suggested that there is a new canon of statutory interpretation so that relevant provisions of UK law can bear a meaning that is consistent with Community law: *Garland v British Rail Engineering Ltd* [1983] 2 AC 751; *McCarthy's Ltd v Wendy Smith* [1979] 3 All ER 325; *Pickstone v Freemans plc* [1988] 2 All ER 803.

More radical approaches are being tentatively adopted which suggest that the duty of the national court is to give effect to Community law in all circumstances: see *R v Secretary of State for Transport ex parte Factortame Ltd and Others* [1989] 2 CMLR 353 CA.

Note that the European Commission brought an action against the UK requiring that the nationality element of the Merchant Shipping Act 1988 be suspended.

e) *Conclusion*

The doctrine of direct applicability and the supremacy of Community law over national rules has led to a surrender of sovereignty on the part of the Westminster Parliament. But while there can be no implied repeal of Community law by national legislation, the position regarding the express repeal of Community law by Act of Parliament is a matter of controversy. While the European Court of Justice maintains that a national court should give effect to Community law even when subsequent national legislation is inconsistent with it, some lawyers argue that the express wish of Parliament must prevail. Two points are however clear:

i) It is only a partial surrender of sovereignty in that it only affects those matters within the competence of the European Community Treaties.

ii) It is only a temporary surrender of sovereignty in that it only applies so long as the European Communities Act 1972 is in force.

4.3 Recent cases and statutes

Single European Act 1986

Pickstone v Freemans plc [1988] 2 All ER 803

4.4 Analysis of questions

The extent to which the UK Parliament remains sovereign becomes an ever more important political question. The legal issue raised in exam questions focuses on the relationship between Community law and UK law where there is a conflict and the approach of the judiciary to such a conflict.

4.5 Question

Parliament wishes to promote affirmative action and decides to allow women to be paid more than men for the same work. It passes the Turning the Tables Act 1987, s1 of which states:

'This Act is to be given effect notwithstanding any decision of the European Court of Justice or any provisions of Community law or any provisions of the European Communities Act 1972.'

Would a British judge still give primacy to Community law if this new Act came into conflict with it?

University of London LLB Examination
(for External Students) Constitutional Law June 1987 Q3

General comment

A relatively simple question concerning the effect of membership of the European Communities on the sovereignty of the Westminster Parliament.

Skeleton solution

- Introduction. The European Communities Act 1972.

- The principles of direct applicability and the supremacy of Community law over national rules. Section 2(1) and s2(4) of the European Communities Act 1972.

- The sovereignty of Parliament. Express repeal and the doctrine of implied repeal. Effect of Community law.

- Effect of parliamentary legislation expressly contrary to Community law. *Macarthy's Ltd* v *Smith* (1979).

- The position with regard to the Turning the Tables Act 1987.

Suggested solution

The United Kingdom became a member of the European Communities with effect from 1 January 1973, by virtue of the Treaty of Accession 1972. For the Treaty of Accession and the Community treaties and law to have legal effect in the United Kingdom it was necessary for Parliament to pass legislation incorporating them into domestic law. This was achieved by the European Communities Act 1972.

The legal regime of the European Community is founded upon the principles of direct applicability rules over conflicting national rules. Certain rules of Community law contained both in the treaties and in regulations made by the Council or the Commission are directly applicable in that, of their own force, they create legal rights and duties enforceable in municipal courts. Community law also forms part of the national law of every member state. The European Court of Justice has held that Community law prevails over national law to the extent that they are inconsistent with one another. These two principles are given effect in the law of the United Kingdom by virtue of s2(1) and s2(4) of the European Communities Act 1972.

By virtue of s2(4) of the European Communities Act 1972 therefore all United Kingdom legislation shall only take effect to the extent that it is consistent with Community law however clearly it may appear from the United Kingdom legislation that it is intended to have effect notwithstanding any Community law to the contrary: *Costa* v *ENEL* (1964); *Amministrazione delle Finanze dello Stato* v *Simmenthal* (1978). It is clear both from the treaty and from statements made by the European Court of Justice that community law should prevail over national law in all circumstances. Any United Kingdom constitutional law doctrine of the legislative sovereignty of Parliament is irrelevant. This approach taken by the European Court of Justice runs completely contrary to the traditional doctrine of the sovereignty of Parliament as enunciated in *Vauxhall Estates Ltd* v *Liverpool Corporation* (1932) and *Ellen Street Estates* v *Minister of Health* (1934). Certainly the doctrine of implied repeal as set out in *Ellen Street Estates* v *Minister of Health*, that later United

Kingdom legislation always, by implication, repeals earlier legislative provisions with which it is inconsistent, would not survive.

But what about the situation such as that under the Turning the Tables Act 1987, where Parliament legislates expressly contrary to Community law. In such a case it may be possible to treat s2(4) as amounting to a rule of interpretation that there shall be a presumption that the United Kingdom Parliament, in passing legislation, intends to legislate consistently with Community law. This approach allows that if the United Kingdom Parliament were to make it clear in a piece of legislation that it intended to legislate contrary to Community law or that it intended the legislation to take effect notwithstanding any provision of Community law to the contrary, then the United Kingdom legislation would prevail over the inconsistent Community law. This is the approach that was favoured by the Court of Appeal in *Macarthy's Ltd v Smith* (1979). A man had been employed as a stockroom keeper at £60 per week. Subsequently a woman was employed in this position at £50 per week. She took the matter to an industrial tribunal on the grounds that this was contrary to law. Two questions arose. Firstly, was this contrary to article 119 of the Treaty of Rome which provides that each member state shall ensure and maintain the application of the principle that men and women should receive equal pay for equal work? Secondly, in the event of a conflict between the United Kingdom legislation and article 119 of the Treaty, which should prevail in English courts?

In the Court of Appeal Lord Denning MR felt that if there were a conflict between the United Kingdom legislation and article 119 of the Treaty, article 119 should prevail since this is required by s2(1) and s2(4) of the European Communities Act 1972. Lord Denning here assumed that Parliament, when it passes legislation, intends to fulfil its obligations under the Treaty. But he felt that if the time should come when Parliament deliberately passes an Act with the intention of repudiating the Treaty or any provision in it or intentionally of acting inconsistently with it and says so in express terms, then it would be the duty of the United Kingdom courts to follow the Act of Parliament. But unless there is such an intentional and express repudiation of the Treaty, it is the duty of the United Kingdom courts to give priority to the Treaty.

Thus Lord Denning put forward the view that if Parliament in an Act stated an express intention to legislate contrary to Community law or notwithstanding Community law, then in that one situation the United Kingdom court would give preference to the United Kingdom legislation over the Community law. This interpretation was also favoured by Lord Diplock in *Garland v British Rail Engineering Ltd* (1983) when he too stated that statutes must be construed in a way consistent with Treaty obligations if they are capable of bearing such a meaning.

This amounts to a retention of the doctrine of express repeal of earlier law by later legislation, but involves the abandonment of the doctrine of implied repeal as far as Community law is concerned. In this approach it is neither consistent with the traditional United Kingdom doctrine of the sovereignty of Parliament, nor with the Community doctrine of the supremacy of Community law over national rules. However, it is yet to be seen how the United Kingdom courts would act if faced with a United Kingdom Act of Parliament expressing an intention of Parliament to legislate contrary to Community law. Regarding the Turning the Tables Act 1987 therefore the position is far from clear. The court may be inclined to uphold the express wish of Parliament and give effect to the Act notwithstanding article 119 of the Treaty of Rome. However the European Court of Justice would almost certainly declare this to be invalid and hold that s1 of the 1987 Act amounts to a blatant repudiation by the United Kingdom of its international obligations under the European Community Treaties.

5 THE ELECTORAL SYSTEM

5.1 Introduction

5.2 Key points

5.3 Recent cases and statutes

5.4 Analysis of questions

5.5 Questions

5.1 Introduction

The membership of the House of Commons is elected on the basis of adult suffrage. A general election must be held at least every five years: Parliament Act 1911.

5.2 Key points

a) *The franchise*

In order to vote in a parliamentary election a person must be included on the electoral register for a parliamentary constituency: Representation of the People Act 1983. To qualify for inclusion a person must:

i) be 18 years of age (or be due to attain his eighteenth birthday within twelve months of the publication of the register);

ii) be a British subject or a citizen of the Republic of Ireland;

iii) not be subject to any legal incapacity;

iv) be resident in the constituency on the qualifying date for compiling the register: *Fox* v *Stirk* [1970] 2 QB 463; *Hipperson* v *Electoral Registration Officer for Newbury* [1985] QB 1060.

b) *Disqualification*

The following persons are not entitled to vote, even if their names appear on the register.

i) Aliens (excluding citizens of the Republic of Ireland)

ii) Minors (persons under 18 years of age)

iii) Peers and peeresses in their own right (Irish peers may vote)

iv) Convicted persons serving sentences of imprisonment

v) Persons convicted of corrupt practices at elections are disqualified from voting for five years. Persons convicted of illegal practices at elections are disqualified from voting for five years in the constituency in question.

vi) Those who for reasons such as mental illness, subnormality or other infirmity lack the capacity at the moment of voting of understanding what they are about to do.

c) *Parliamentary constituencies*

The United Kingdom is divided into constituencies each of which is represented by a Member in the House of Commons.

i) Constituency boundaries are delimited by the Boundary Commissioners.

ii) The basic principle that each constituency should have the same number of electors is to ensure that all votes have equal value.

Quota = no. of electors divided by no. of constituencies

iii) Boundary Commissioners have discretion to depart from strict application of the rules if there are special geographical or other considerations that render departure desirable: House of Commons Redistribution of Seats Acts 1949-79; see too Schedule II.

iv) The re-drawing of the constituency map can result in challenges: *R v Boundary Commission for England ex parte Foot* [1983] 1 All ER 1099; *Harper v Home Secretary* [1955] Ch 238; *R v Home Secretary ex parte McWhirter* [1969] CLY 2636.

d) *Electoral Campaign*

i) It is an offence to incur expenditure 'with a view to promoting or procuring the election of a candidate at an election' without authorisation of the candidate or his agent for public meetings and displays and advertisements or 'otherwise presenting to the electorate the candidate or his views or the extent or nature of his backing or disparaging another candidate': s75 Representation of the People Act 1983.

ii) There are limits placed on the amount a candidate can spend: s76 Representation of the People Act 1983; *R v Hailwood* [1928] 2 KB 277; *R v Tronoh Mines* [1952] 1 All ER 697; *Grieve v Douglas Home* (1965) SC 315; *DPP v Luft* [1976] 2 All ER 569.

e) *Broadcasts*

i) Party political broadcast: *Evans v BBC & IBA* [1974] CLY 434

ii) Other broadcasts: *Marshall v BBC* [1979] 3 All ER 80

f) *The election of Members of Parliament*

At present Members of Parliament are elected under the simple majority voting system. Each parliamentary constituency returns a single member. Each elector can vote for one candidate only and the candidate who polls the most votes within a given constituency wins the seat.

i) Disadvantages of the simple majority voting systems

- There are many wasted votes.

- It is a very crude system.

- There is no relationship between the number of votes cast nationally for a particular party and the number of seats allocated to that party in the House of Commons.

- The system produces exaggerated majorities for the two major parties and discriminates against the minority parties.

ii) Advantages of the simple majority voting system

- The voting procedure is simple and the results may be quickly calculated.

- There is a link between the member and his constituency.

- One party usually obtains an absolute majority of seats in the House of Commons thus leading to strong government.

g) *Electoral reform*

The three main alternatives to our present system are:

i) The Alternative Vote. Voters list the candidates in order of preference. If no candidate gains an absolute majority of first preference votes then the lowest candidate is eliminated and his second preference votes are distributed among the other candidates. The process may be repeated until a candidate emerges who has an absolute majority.

ii) The Party List System. One constituency comprising the whole country. The parties present lists of candidates and electors vote not for individual candidates but for the whole party list. Seats are then allocated to the parties in proportion to the votes received by each party list.

iii) The Single Transferable Vote. Requires multi-member constituencies of between five and seven members. Voters list the candidates in order of preference. The candidate needs a quota of votes to be elected. Any votes he receives beyond this figure are surplus and so they are redistributed among the other candidates according to second preference. The quota is usually established by the following formula:

number of votes cast + 1
number of seats + 1

5.3   Recent cases and statutes

Representation of the People Act 1983

Representation of the People Act 1985

Parliamentary Constituencies Act 1986

Hipperson v *Electoral Registration Officer for Newbury* [1985] QB 1060

R v *Boundary Commission for England ex parte Foot* [1983] QB 600

5.4 Analysis of questions

Questions on this area seem to be set when the subject is topical ie just before or just after an election. Examiners favour essay type questions on the voting system in the UK - its advantages and disadvantages - a question that requires students to have some knowledge of alternative systems.

Students need to be aware of the role of the Boundary Commissioners and the problems that can arise when they report.

Problem questions could be set on the rules governing elections.

5.5 Questions

QUESTION 1

a) What is the function of the Boundary Commission and what problems can occur when it reports?

b) Rupert is a newspaper proprietor. He stood as candidate for the Freedom Party at a general election. His newspapers carried advertisements extolling the virtues of the Freedom Party and urging people to vote for it. Rupert was elected.

Blake, a constituent, seeks to challenge Rupert's election as MP on the grounds that he incurred unauthorised expenditure.

Discuss.

Written by Editor February 1990

General comment

An easy question if students know the cases and statutes below.

Skeleton solution

a) • The function of the Boundary Commission - House of Commons Redistribution of Seats Acts 1949-79.

   • An explanation of the effect on political parties when constituencies are redefined.

   R v *Boundary Commission for England ex parte Foot* (1983)

b) • The provisions of s75 Representation of the People Act 1983.

   • An analysis of cases on unauthorised expenditure: *R* v *Tronoh Mines* (1952); *Grieve* v *Douglas Home* (1965); *DPP* v *Luft* (1976).

Suggested solution

a) The function of the Boundary Commission as laid down by the House of Commons Redistribution of Seats Acts is to regulate the size of parliamentary constituencies in the United Kingdom. The purpose is to achieve, as far as is practicable, constituencies which are approximately equal in terms of voters. A figure is arrived at by dividing the number of voters by the number of constituencies which produces a current figure of approximately 65,000.

The commissioners do have, however, discretionary powers to vary the size of constituencies taking into account county boundaries and special geographical considerations including the size, shape and accessibility of a constituency. In the exercise of their discretion the commissioners should observe a balance between the countries of the UK ie Great Britain should not have substantially more or less seats than 613, Scotland should not have less than 71, Wales 31 and Northern Ireland between 16 and 18.

Under their powers the commissioners present their recommendations to the Home Secretary whose duty it is to lay these before Parliament for approval. The objective is to remove the decision from the political process because changes are perceived by one party or another as disadvantaging them and political agreement is therefore unlikely. The only circumstances in which a review of their decision is likely is if 100 or more affected voters petition or if a County Council petitions. The only other way is to challenge through judicial review the exercise of the commissioners' discretion.

The Labour party has traditionally been disadvantaged by changes largely because of migration from urban areas, traditionally labour strongholds, to the country. In the late 1960s the Labour Party sought to delay the implementation of proposals: see *R* v *Home Secretary ex parte McWhirter* (1969). More recently Foot, then leader of the Labour Party, sought to challenge the proposals on the grounds that the commissioners had exercised their powers wrongly and that the decision was ultra vires: *R* v *Boundary Commission for England ex parte Foot* (1983). The court held that the discretion of the commissioners was very wide and that they had not acted unreasonably. The challenge failed.

b)   Section 75 of the Representation of the People Act 1983 makes it an offence to incur expenditure with a view to promoting or procuring the election of a candidate at an election without the authority of the candidate or his agent and s76 goes on to place limits on the candidate's expenditure. The amount is varied from time to time by means of statutory instrument. The objective here is to ensure that one candidate does not gain advantage by virtue of the fact that he may have substantial personal wealth to wage a campaign and can be contrasted with other countries notably America where there are no limits.

There are however no limits in this country on the amount that a national party can spend on a campaign. It can be argued that this is a disadvantage to some political parties, more particularly the smaller parties whose ability to wage a national campaign is limited by a lack of money. It is a tradition in this country that political parties grow out of grass roots support. The issue in the question therefore would seem to be simply whether the newspaper advertisement can be seen as essentially part of a national campaign or whether the intention and effect is to ensure the election of the local candidate Rupert.

In support of the principle that expenditure incurred cannot exceed the permitted maximum it has been held that a local campaign urging the electorate not to vote for a particular candidate falls foul of s75 because by implication it is of advantage to the other: see *DPP* v *Luft* (1976). However on the question of national newspaper campaigns it has been held that an advertisement advocating the defeat of a Labour government was not an election expense within the meaning of s75: see *R* v *Tronoh Mines* (1952). Furthermore, in *Grieve* v *Douglas Home* (1965), an unsuccessful Communist candidate who argued that Douglas Home the then Prime Minister gained an unfair advantage in respect of his local campaign when he appeared on national television did not convince the courts. Such a broadcast was not held to be expenditure with a view to procuring his election.

By analogy then it would seem unlikely that Blake would be successful in his challenge unless the advertisement referred to in the problem specifically relates to Rupert's own campaign. Whilst he may gain some advantage from such an advertisement, on the facts the advertisement is aimed at furthering the interests of the party nationally.

QUESTION 2

What difference, if any, would reforming the electoral system make to the British Constitution?

Written by Editor February 1990

General comment

This is a very straightforward question involving discussion of the present electoral system and the effect reform would have on the British Constitution.

Skeleton solution

• Introduction. The operation of the relative majority system.

• The problems with the present system. Parliamentary seats not allocated on a proportional basis; discrimination against small parties; wastage of votes; problems with constituency size.

• The advantages of the present system. Simplicity; results in strong government; constituency link with MP.

• Effect of reform. Loss of the advantages of the present system; election of a Parliament but not a government.

Suggested solution

Under the present parliamentary electoral system the United Kingdom is divided into 650 parliamentary constituencies, each of which returns a single member to the House of Commons. Each elector may vote for one candidate only and the successful

35

candidate is the one who receives the highest number of valid votes in the constituency. This system of 'first past the post' is known as the simple majority system as wherever there are more than two candidates in a constituency, the successful candidate need not have received an absolute majority of votes, but simply a majority over the runner-up. This system has the advantage of being very simple, but as a means of providing representation of the electorate in Parliament it is very crude. It is a system which, according to its critics, is not truly democratic and one which has several inherent disadvantages which, it is argued, can only be overcome by reform.

Certainly any reform of the present electoral system will seek to remedy the major problem that at present the system does not ensure that the distribution of seats in the House of Commons is in any way proportionate to the national distribution of votes. There is no consistent relationship between the number of votes cast nationally for a political party and the seats which they obtain. This is well illustrated by the June 1983 election results. The Conservative Party polled 42.4 per cent of the votes cast and won 397 seats. The Labour Party rolled 27.6 per cent of the votes cast and won 209 seats. But the Liberal/SDP Alliance polled 25.4 per cent of the votes cast and won only 23 seats. The Alliance therefore was under-represented in relation to their national vote, while the Conservative Government achieved the largest parliamentary majority since the war, but received one of the smallest percentages of votes cast. Under this system a Conservative vote thus carried more weight than an Alliance vote.

This tendency of the system to exaggerate the representation of the large parties and reduce that of the smaller parties leads to the allegation that the present electoral system makes no provision for the representation of minority interests. It discriminates against the smaller parties whose support is evenly spread throughout the country rather than being concentrated in particular constituencies. Votes for the smaller parties are, in effect, wasted votes. It doesn't matter whether the person elected has one more or twenty thousand more votes than his nearest rival. So where there are more than two candidates a person may be elected by less than 50 per cent of the total votes cast in that constituency. The votes for the losing candidate have no parliamentary importance, they are in a sense wasted. This system, it is argued, perpetuates the two party system and helps destroy any possibility of consensus politics in the United Kingdom.

A further problem arises from the constituency basis of the present system. If votes are to carry equal weight throughout the country each constituency must be of equal size. The size of every constituency is determined by the Boundary Commissioners who keep the situation under constant review and try to ensure that each constituency has the same number of voters in it. However disparity does exist between constituency populations and as a result the weight of your vote may vary according to where you live.

Reforming the electoral system would therefore help remove these problems and help achieve fairer representation for all political parties in the House of Commons. But it must always be remembered that the present electoral system has considerable advantages and that these advantages may be lost as a result of any reform. For example the voting procedure itself is very simple and easy to understand, ensuring quick results. The outcome of the election is known within a matter of hours of the close of poll. However disparity does exist between constituency populations and as a result the weight of your vote may vary according to where you live.

Reforming the electoral system would therefore help remove these problems and help achieve fairer representation for all political parties in the House of Commons. But it must always be remembered that the present electoral system has considerable advantages and that these advantages may be lost as a result of any reform. For example the voting procedure itself is very simple and easy to understand, ensuring quick results. The outcome of the election is known within a matter of hours of the close of poll. The system also ensures a close link between the Member of Parliament and his constituency. The constituents know who their parliamentary representative is and can approach him with their problems. He in turn will serve their interests, in the knowledge that their continued support is necessary if he is to be re-elected.

But the major advantage claimed for the present system is its tendency to produce an absolute majority of seats in the House of Commons for one party. The function of a general election is to elect a government as well as a parliament and the present system does precisely that, producing strong government. The United Kingdom system avoids the problems, often found in European countries, which use different electoral systems, of coalition or minority governments which can find it difficult to govern effectively because of their unstable electoral position.

Despite these advantages there is a case for reforming the electoral system so as to secure better representation of minority parties and a distribution of seats which bears some relation to the votes cast. The most favoured alternative systems are the alternative vote system, the party list system and the single transferable vote system. The adoption of any one of these systems would bring about changes to the British Constitution which, while welcomed by some, would be abhorrent to others.

The major result of adopting these systems is that they will help achieve legislative representation which accords with the relative electoral strengths of the political parties. Minority parties and independent candidates will therefore stand a better chance of election and the number of wasted votes will be reduced. But while these systems may to an extent maintain a local basis for representation, they may weaken the link between Members of Parliament and constituents. These systems of election are also complex. Most important, however, is the likely result that the traditional two party system may be destroyed. To some of course this may be no bad thing but, if the European experience is repeated and one party is less likely to secure an absolute majority of seats in the House of Commons, this will lead to minority or coalition governments giving smaller parties political importance out of all proportion to their popular support. Such a system of government is totally alien to the British tradition.

QUESTION 3

Explain the advantages and disadvantages of:

a) the present British electoral system; and

b) any one alternative.

University of London LLB Examination
(for External Students) Constitutional Law June 1984 Q2

General comment

A relatively easy and straightforward question asking for the advantages and disadvantages of the present simple majority electoral system and any one alternative. It is simply a matter of describing and explaining the operation of the present system, followed by a detached analysis of its advantages and disadvantages. The same with the alternative.

There are several alternative systems based upon the idea of proportional representation that could be chosen - but remember that some are very complex and difficult to describe. In this respect, the single transferable vote system is probably the best alternative to choose.

Do remember that while one mostly hears criticisms of the present electoral system voiced in the media, nevertheless it does have considerable advantages. Indeed if your disadvantages outweigh your advantages, something is missing.

Skeleton solution

• Outline of voting system in the UK.

• The consequences - advantages and disadvantages - of the 'first past the post' method of electing MPs.

• An explanation of an alternative method, eg single transferable vote or the alternative vote with an analysis of the effect on the composition of the House of Commons.

Suggested solution

Under the present parliamentary electoral system the United Kingdom is divided into 650 parliamentary constituencies, each of which returns a single member to the House of Commons. Each elector may vote for one candidate only and the successful candidate is the one who receives the highest number of valid votes in the constituency. This system of 'first past the post' is known as the simple majority system as whenever there are more than two candidates in a constituency, the successful candidate need not have received an absolute majority of votes, but simply a majority over the runner up. This system has the advantage of being very simple, but as a means of providing representation of the electorate in Parliament it is very crude. It is a system which, according to its critics, is not truly democratic and one which has several inherent disadvantages.

The major criticism is that the system does not ensure that the distribution of seats in the House of Commons is in any way proportionate to the national distribution of votes. There is no consistent relationship between the number of votes and the seats which they obtain. This is aptly illustrated by the June 1983 election results. The Conservatives polled 42.4 per cent of the votes cast and won 397 seats. The Labour party polled 27.6 per cent of the votes cast and won 209 seats. But the Liberal/SDP Alliance polled 25.4 per cent of the votes cast and won only 23 seats. The Alliance therefore was under-represented in relation to their national votes, while the Conservative government achieved the largest parliamentary majority since the war, but received one of the smallest percentages of votes cast. Under this system a Conservative vote thus carried more weight than an Alliance vote.

The tendency of the system to exaggerate the representation of the large parties and reduce that of the smaller parties leads to an allegation that the system makes no provision for the representation of minority interests. It discriminates against the smaller parties whose support is evenly spread throughout the country rather than being concentrated in particular constituencies. Votes for the smaller parties are, in effect, wasted votes. It doesn't matter whether the person elected has one more or twenty thousand more votes than his nearest rival. So where there are more than two candidates a person may be elected by less than 50 per cent of the total votes cast in that constituency. The votes for the losing candidate have no parliamentary importance, they are in a sense wasted.

A further problem arises from the constituency basis of the present system. If votes are to carry equal weight throughout the country each constituency must be of equal size. The size of each constituency is determined by the Boundary Commissioners who keep the situation under constant review and try to ensure that each constituency has the same number of voters in it. However, disparity does exist between constituency populations and as a result the weight of your vote may vary according to where you live.

Against these criticisms must be weighed the advantages of the present system. The voting procedure itself is very simple and easy to understand, ensuring quick results. The outcome of the election is known within a matters of hours of the close of poll. The system also ensures a close link between the Member of Parliament and his constituency. The constituents know who their parliamentary representative is and can approach him with their problems. He in turn will serve their interests, in the knowledge that their continued support is necessary if he is to be re-elected.

The major advantage claimed for the present system is its tendency to produce an absolute majority of seats in the House of Commons for one party. The function of a general election is to elect a government as well as a Parliament and the present system does produce strong government. The United Kingdom system avoids the problems, often found in European countries, which use different electoral systems, of coalition or minority governments which can find it difficult to govern effectively because of their unstable electoral position.

Despite these advantages there is a case for reforming the electoral system so as to secure better representation of minority parties and a distribution of seats which bears some relation to the votes cast. One alternative which is likely to produce a more proportional system of representation is the single transferable vote. Under this system the country would be divided into multi-member constituencies, each returning between three and seven members. Each elector would have a single vote, but he would vote for candidates in order of preference. Any candidate obtaining the quota of first preference votes necessary to guarantee election would be immediately elected, the quota being calculated by a simple formula: eg in a five member constituency, the quota would be one vote more than one-sixth of the total votes cast. The surplus votes of a successful candidate would be distributed to other candidates proportionately according to the second preference expressed. Any candidate obtaining the quota would be elected and a similar distribution of his surplus would follow. If at any count no candidate obtained the quota figure, the candidate with the lowest number of votes would be eliminated and all his votes redistributed amongst the others.

The major advantages of this system is that it achieves legislative representation which accords with the relative electoral strengths of the political parties. Minority parties and independent candidates would stand a better chance of election and the number of wasted votes would be reduced.

But while the system maintains a local basis for representation, it weakens the link between Members of Parliament and constituents. The system of election is also complex. Most important, however, if the European experience is repeated, one party will be less likely to secure an absolute majority of seats in the House of Commons, leading to minority or coalition governments giving smaller parties political importance out of proportion to their popular support.

QUESTION 4

Comment on the following: 'The British electoral system is based on the slogan "one man, one vote" but in certain important ways each vote is not of equal value.'

University of London LLB Examination
(for External Students) Constitutional Law June 1983 Q3

General comment

This question asks students to criticise the electoral system as it stands and not just to suggest different reforms that could be brought in. However, the word 'comment' allows students a degree of lee-way as to which direction the answer should go, so there is no right and wrong.

You should start with a description of the present system and state that there have been suggestions of reform throughout the century. Then give a fairly detailed analysis of why the system maybe undemocratic including percentage of vote, Boundary Commission etc, and then suggest alternatives - party list systems etc. In conclusion perhaps you would like to mention the views of the main parties on the topic and mention the advantages of the present system. Statistics are not needed in the answer but it would help if you remembered some - perhaps of the June 1983 election.

Skeleton solution

* Outline of voting system in UK.

* The constitutional problems: all votes do not carry the same weight as constituencies are unequal in numbers of electors; percentage of votes cast for each party does not equal the numbers of seats gained.

* Alternatives and consequences for the British political system.

Suggested solution

At present Members of Parliament are elected on the simple basis that within a given constituency the person who polls the most votes wins. This is the 'one man one vote' or 'first past the post' system or more properly election by relative majority. Throughout the last century there have been calls for reform of this system as it is felt not to be truly democratic. Recently there was a surge of public interest in electoral reform which partly arose from the temporary emergence of the Social Democratic Party as a political force. Electoral reform continues to be on the political agenda but not as a priority. The two major parties have again consolidated their position.

The first reason for suggesting that not all votes carry the same weight follows from the actual number of voters in each constituency. The size of each constituency is determined by one of the four Boundary Commissions. As a basic principle each constituency should have the same number of voters in it. However, a Boundary Commission is entitled to depart from the strict application of this principle if 'special geographical considerations' so require. The rearrangement of the constituencies can have important effects on the political 'colour' of a given area. There was such a rearrangement prior to the 1983 election which the Labour Party unsuccessfully challenged in the courts: *R* v *Boundary Commissioners for England ex parte Foot* (1983). This has been given as one of the reasons for the increased Tory majority. In the case of *Baker* v *Carr* (1962) the US Supreme Court ruled that where the State of Tennessee had failed to provide constituencies of the equal average population that was a breach of the fourteenth amendment to the Constitution. Prior to the 1983 rearrangement the smallest constituency in the United Kingdom had about a quarter of the population of the largest. It can be said that the weight of your vote varies according to where you live.

The problems of varying size of constituency can to some extent be overcome. However the greatest failing of a relative majority system, and perhaps this is what makes it undemocratic, is that the percentage of votes cast throughout the country for a particular party do not reflect the number of seats it receives in the House of Commons. One need only look at the percentage share of votes compared to seats in recent elections. In 1979 Conservatives took 339 seats from 44 per cent of the votes. Labour took 268 seats from 37 per cent and the Liberals took 11 seats from 14 per cent of the votes. The situation was particularly highlighted in the 1983 election results. The Conservatives took 397 seats from 42.4 per cent, the Labour Party took

209 from 27.6 per cent of the votes and the Alliance took 23 from 25.4 per cent. This distortion created by the process of translating votes into seats has become a matter of some public concern. Under this system a vote for Conservative in 1983 had more weight than a vote for an Alliance candidate. Both election results suggest that when talking to a stranger it is more likely he did not vote for the present government than he did! In the 1983 election the Conservatives scored against the Alliance by reason of the favour the system bestows upon the largest party when confronted by nearly equally divided opposition. The Labour Party and the Ulster Unionists scored by reason of the favour bestowed on a party whose support is more concentrated than dispersed. The gross deformity in results in the 1983 election may be temporary during a transition in opposition or abortive challenge to the two party system. As it stands however the weight of a vote varies with the party for which it is cast.

The relative majority system means that no account is taken of the size of a majority. A Tory MP returned with a 30,000 majority is of equal status to a Labour MP returned with a majority of three. So all votes cast in the above example over the total necessary to defeat the other candidates are in a sense wasted and of no parliamentary importance.

There is obviously a case for reforming the electoral system with a view to reducing the discrepancy between votes cast for and seats won by a party campaigning on a national scale. The most favoured systems around the world are the alternative vote system, the party list system and the single transferable vote.

The introduction of an alternative vote system would require little change save for the voter placing the candidates in order of preference on the ballot paper. If no candidate obtains an absolute majority by counting first preferences, the candidate at the bottom of the poll is eliminated, and his second preference votes are distributed among the other candidates, and so on until one candidate has more than 50 per cent. The result may be that the candidate placed second on the first count wins the seats. This system is not a proportional system. Sir Winston Churchill dismissed it as being 'the worst of all possible plans in which the decision is to be determined by the most worthless votes given to the most worthless candidate', and one can see his point!

The only precise means of achieving direct proportionality is to have the country as one constituency with the parties presenting list of candidates and electors voting not for individual candidates but for the whole party list. Seats are then allocated to the parties in proportion to the votes received by each party. Under our present system although in theory people vote for the candidate they think will best represent them in Parliament in practice people vote for a party. The introduction of a party list system would merely confirm this practice. However it would pose difficulties in drawing up the list in particular the order of the candidates and it would destroy the territorial constituency system with its strong link between one MP and one constituency.

The Single Transferable Vote System (STV) is an alternative to the party list. It requires multi-member constituencies (five to seven members) and voters list the individual candidates in order of preference. In counting the votes the principle that applies is that a candidate only needs a certain number and any surplus votes are redistributed among the other candidates according to second preferences. The quota is usually the number of votes cast divided by the number of seats but there are several variations in procedure throughout the world. STV is used in Australia and Eire and many trade unions and professional organisations use it to elect their National Committees. The introduction of this system would produce a more representative House of Commons. This system of proportional representation is described as the 'linchpin of the entire programme of reform' outlined in the 1983 Alliance manifesto. They feel that the first past the post system ensures the under-representation of all those who reject class as the basis of politics and that reform is necessary for democracy. It is probably also necessary for the Alliance to obtain power in the present political climate. The criticisms of STV are that it may not and usually does not produce a government with a working majority, it breaks up the local constituency and produces coalition governments with a consequent blurring of policy alternatives on major issues. Supporters of STV would say that this last was its strongest point and that polarisation and reversal politics of successions of Labour and Tory governments are not in the best interests of the country as a whole.

Whatever the arguments on either side the fact is that the suggestion that votes are of unequal value in the present system is obviously correct. But it begs the question - what makes a satisfactory electoral system? An electoral system reflects each country's politics of which it is both cause and effect. Majority voting is usually the norm in a two-party system, proportional representation in a multi-party system. The overriding requirement is that it is seen to be reasonable by the country to ensure the best representation possible and may be in particular to safeguard the representation of minorities. One might think that a quarter of the population are at present under-represented in the House of Commons.

6   LEGISLATURE I - THE HOUSE OF COMMONS

6.1 Introduction

6.2 Key points

6.3 Recent cases and statutes

6.4 Analysis of questions

6.5 Questions

6.1   Introduction

The monarch is one of the three constituent parts of the legislature but the role of the monarchy is now largely ceremonial and formal. The United Kingdom has a bicameral legislature - there are two Houses of Parliament - the House of Commons and the House of Lords. The House of Commons dominates.

The central issue relating to the legislature is one of accountability of government. The House of Commons is dominated by the government particularly if following a general election the government has a large majority. The House of Lords is seen by many as performing, amongst its other functions, that of challenging the government at a political level on unpopular policies. However, ultimately the Commons can successfully achieve its political will in the unlikely event of a confrontation.

Text book analysis of the topic describes the rules and procedures of the House of Commons. Students must be able to place this knowledge in the context of executive power and understand the nature of the relationship between government and the Commons - see chapter nine: *The Executive* and chapter 10: *The Royal Prerogative*.

6.2   Key points

The main functions of Parliament include the passing of legislation and the scrutiny of the administration through debate, the committee system and the control of national finance.

a)   *The legislative process*

i)   A distinction must be drawn between Public and Private Bills:

- Public Bills seek to alter the general law and affect the whole community.

- Private Bills affect only a section of the community and relate to matters of individual, corporate or local interest.

- Hybrid Bills are Public Bills that are classified by the Speaker as having a particular effect on one section of the community.

ii)   Public Bill procedure

Most Public Bills are Government Bills, but some may be Private Members Bills introduced by backbench Members of Parliament. Bills may be introduced into either House, but legislation which is politically controversial, financial or electoral begins in the House of Commons.

- First reading: The Bill is presented to Parliament.

- Second reading: The House considers the principle and merits of the Bill.

- Committee stage: The Bill is normally referred to a standing committee for detailed clause by clause consideration.

- Report stage: The Bill as amended is reported to the whole House.

- Third reading: The Bill is debated in general terms with only oral amendments allowed.

- House of Lords stages and amendments: After its third reading, the Bill is sent to the House of Lords where it goes through stages similar to those in the Commons. But note the effects of the Parliament Acts 1911-1949.

- Royal assent: Now a formality. After the Royal Assent has been given the Bill becomes an Act.

iii) Private Member's Bill procedure

There are a number of procedures under which Private Members may initiate Bills.

- The Ballot: The Ballot establishes an order of priority enabling those Members successful in it to use the limited Private Members' time for debate of their Bills which, given the governments' control of the parliamentary timetable, might otherwise not make progress.

- The Ten Minute Rule: Not, in general, serious attempts at legislation. The Member may speak briefly in support of the Bill and an opponent may reply. The House may then decide on whether the Bill should be introduced.

- Standing Order No 39: Allows every Member the right to introduce a Bill of his choosing after due notice.

iv) Private Bill procedure

Private Bills are initiated by petition from persons or bodies outside Parliament. Full notice must be given to those whose legal rights may be affected by the proposed legislation so that they may oppose it. In the House of Commons the Bill is introduced by being presented at the Table by the Clerk of the Private Bill Office. It is then deemed to have been read for the first time. At the Second Reading Debate, the House determines whether the Bill is unobjectionable from the point of view of national policy. If read a second time, the Bill is committed to a committee of four Members in the Commons (or five Members in the Lords). The committee stage has some of the features of a quasi-judicial proceeding.

v) Hybrid Bill procedure

The Standing Orders for private business apply to a hybrid Bill so that if opposed after its second reading it goes before a Select Committee, where those whose legal rights are affected by the Bill may raise their objections and petition against it. After the petitioners have been heard by the Select Committee, the Bill then passes through its committee stage and later stages as if it were an ordinary Bill.

b) *Opportunities for debate in the House of Commons*

Apart from the opportunities for debate during the legislative process, there are various other opportunities for debate in the House of Commons.

i) Adjournment debates

At the end of every day's business, when the adjournment of the House is formally moved, half an hour is made available for a private Member to raise a topic in debate and for a ministerial reply to be given.

ii) Standing Order No 10 - Motion to Adjourn

This allows Members to suggest that a specific and important matter should have urgent consideration and that an emergency debate be held upon it.

iii) Other opportunities

The final day before each of the four parliamentary recesses is also devoted to a series of Private Members' debates and ten Fridays per session are also set aside for Private Members' Motions. Other opportunities for debate occur in the debate on the address in reply to the Queen's Speech, the debate on the Budget, debates on motions of censure, the twenty Opposition Days, the three Estimate Days and on the second reading of Consolidated Fund Bills.

iv) Devices for curtailing debate

Delay of Bills in the House of Commons is a threat to the government's legislative programme. To overcome this threat, various methods of curtailing debate have been adopted by the House.

- Standing Order 22: The Speaker or Chairman may require a Member to discontinue his speech if he persists in irrelevance or tedious repetition.

- The Closure: Any Member may move 'that the question now be put'. If not less than 100 members vote for the motion the debate ceases and the motion under discussion must be voted upon.

- The Kangaroo: This is the power of the Speaker at the Report Stage to select from amongst the various proposed amendments those which are to be discussed.

- The Guillotine Motion: Such a motion provides that one or more stages of a Bill be disposed of either by a fixed date, or by a fixed number of sittings.

c)   *Parliamentary questions*

There are three categories of question:

i)   Question for oral answer which is intended to be given an oral answer in the House during Question Time.

ii) Private notice question which can be asked if the Speaker judges its subject matter to be urgent and important. These are taken orally in the House at the end of Question Time.

iii) Question for written answer, which is not taken orally in the House but is printed in the official report (Hansard).

d)   *Parliamentary committees*

The committees of the House of Commons fall into two main categories:

i)   Standing committees

These are responsible for the committee stage in the passing of a Bill.

ii) Select committees

• Ad-hoc select committees: These are set up for a specific purpose when the need arises.

• Sessional select committees: These are set up at the beginning of the session and remain throughout the session.

• Departmental select committees: These are appointed to examine the expenditure, administration and policy of the principal government departments and associated public bodies.

e)   *Parliamentary control of national finance*

Parliamentary control of national finance has two aspects:

i)   Parliamentary control of government expenditure

• Estimate Days: There are now three annual days devoted to consideration of the main and Supplementary Estimates.

• The Public Accounts Committee: This is a select committee concerned with public money already spent, to see that it has been spent economically, and not wastefully.

• National Audit Act 1983: This Act provides for the appointment of the Comptroller and Auditor General, establishing a Public Accounts Commission and a National Audit Office and making new provisions for promoting economy, efficiency and effectiveness in the use of public money by government departments and other authorities and bodies.

ii) Control over taxation

- Budget Resolutions and the Finance Bill: These provide an opportunity for Members to debate government proposals for taxation and duties etc.

6.3 Recent cases and statutes

Students need to follow the passage of contentious legislation and listen to, watch and/or read reports of debates during any parliamentary session to best understand the way in which the House of Commons operates in practice and to give immediacy to their studies. Recent examples include: Education Reform Act 1988; Local Government Finance Act 1988.

6.4 Analysis of questions

Questions are essay type. They tend to examine the student's understanding of the relationship between government and the legislature and so require a broadly based knowledge which includes the separation of powers, conventions of the Constitution and Cabinet government.

6.5 Questions

QUESTION 1

The parliamentary function of legislation has effectively passed to the Cabinet.

Discuss.

University of London LLB Examination
(for External Students) Constitutional Law June 1986 Q5

General comment

This question revolves around the old argument as to whether Parliament legislates or merely legitimates Executive policy. As well as examining the role of the backbench MP and the House of Lords in the legislative process, students should also consider whether in fact today legislation is not so much decided by the Cabinet as the Prime Minister.

Skeleton solution

- Introduction: the enactment of legislation by the Queen in Parliament.

- The House of Commons: does it legislate or merely legitimate; the control of the Commons by the Executive.

- The role of the House of Lords: the ability of the Lords to check the Executive.

- The role of the backbench MP: Private Members' Bills.

- Conclusion: Cabinet legislation or Prime Ministerial legislation.

Suggested Solution

For purposes of constitutional analysis, the functions of government have often been divided into three broad classes - legislative, executive and judicial. The legislative function involves the enactment of general rules determining the structure and powers of public authorities and regulating the conduct of citizens and private organisations. In the United Kingdom, legislative authority is vested in the Queen in Parliament: new law being enacted when it has been approved by Commons and Lords and has received the Royal Assent.

The passing of legislation therefore is one of the primary functions of Parliament. Bills, which may be either public or private, cannot become law until they have been passed by Parliament and received the Royal Assent. However many consider that Parliament no longer legislates but rather that it merely legitimates proposed legislation already decided upon by the Executive. Certainly, the great majority of Public Bills are prepared for Parliament by the government, which is also responsible for supervising their passage through each House. The Executive therefore participates actively in the process of legislation. Party domination of the House of Commons and the use of the whip system ensures that, generally speaking, when the government has a working majority in the Commons, no new legislation can be enacted by Parliament which is not approved also by the government and that those Bills which are approved are passed.

There are however occasions when in spite of the government's control of the Commons its Members may exert their independence and refuse to act as a mere rubber stamp for Executive policy. For example the Commons effectively blocked attempts by the Labour government to reform the House of Lords in 1968 and attempts by Mrs Thatcher to reform the law on Sunday trading were defeated following a backbench Conservative revolt in the Commons. One must also remember that Parliament also includes the House of Lords and that although the legislative powers of the Lords have been severely curtailed under the Parliament Acts of 1911 and 1949 the chamber, retaining as it does a large degree of political independence, may still act as an effective check on Government Bills.

Although the House of Lords no longer has power over money matters, under the Parliament Acts their Lordships do retain the power to amend non-money Bills and although the House cannot impose its will on the Commons in legislation, it can effectively delay Government Bills for one year. In practice therefore where the government has a heavy legislative programme amendment or delay in the Lords can seriously threaten the legislative timetable for that particular session and the government will be forced to take notice and attempt a compromise with the Lords. If compromise fails and the government implements the procedure under the Parliament Acts, even a one year delay may prove fatal to the government's plans. Recent events have illustrated how the House of Lords can exert its independence and challenge government legislation. The Local Government Finance Act 1988 and the Education Reform Act 1988 both were amended by the House of Lords. It must however be conceded that a determined government will successfully achieve its purpose in the face of the House of Lords. Mrs Thatcher's first administration sustained 45 defeats in their Lordships' Chamber.

It must also be remembered that not all Public Bills are initiated by the Executive. Although the bulk of the legislative programme of Parliament is taken up by

Government Bills, a small but significant part of the programme consists of Bills introduced by backbench MPs. Although the scope for legislative initiative by individual MPs is severely limited, both because of restricted parliamentary time and of the tight hold which the government maintains over departmental responsibilities, standing orders, while generally giving precedence to government business, nevertheless set aside ten Fridays in each session on which Private Members' Bills have priority. The fact that not many of these Bills reach the statute book does not detract from their value as expressions of the independent legislative function of Parliament.

However, in spite of the opportunities for Private Members to introduce their Bills, the independence of the House of Lords and the occasional rebellion amongst backbench members of the government party in the House of Commons, it is probably true to say that in the main the parliamentary function of legislation has effectively passed to the Cabinet, at least in the sense that the Cabinet is the core of collective responsibility.

Traditionally it is in the Cabinet where government policy is thrashed out before being put to Parliament for what has largely become the formality of approval. However this may not necessarily be the case today. We are experiencing a period of prime ministerial government where policy decisions are made by the Prime Minister and her small inner-Cabinet based largely upon the advice of Cabinet committees and the Prime Minister's own policy unit. The full Cabinet, if consulted at all, merely approves whatever is put before it. It may therefore, at least for the time being, be more accurate to say that the parliamentary function of legislation has effectively passed to the Prime Minister.

QUESTION 2

Evaluate the following statement:

'A serious weakness of the House of Commons is the ineffectual role of so many backbenchers.' (de Smith)

University of London LLB Examination
(for External Students) Constitutional Law June 1984 Q3

General comment

In this question de Smith is commenting upon the fact that backbench MPs have opportunities available to scrutinise Government policy but that because of the procedure of the Commons and the stranglehold of the Government over the legislative system, these opportunities are mostly ineffectual. However, following this quote in his *Constitutional and Administrative Law* de Smith goes on to describe the success of the select committees in increasing the effectiveness of backbench MPs. Students, in evaluating the statement, should therefore weigh against the traditional factors limiting the effectiveness of the backbench MP in the Chamber, the success and achievements of the new specialist select committees. Mention should also be made of the anticipated benefits to the backbenchers' role following the passing of the National Audit Act.

Skeleton solution

- Introduction - an outline of the opportunities available to backbenchers to participate in the business of the House of Commons.

- Examination of the system of select committees including their function.

- Limitations of select committees and the role of backbenchers.

- Conclusion - evaluation of the backbenchers' role.

Suggested solution

The role of any backbenchers in the scrutiny of government policy and administration is largely ineffectual. Backbenchers have their opportunities to call the government to account on the occasions set aside for Private Members' Motions, on the motions for the adjournment each day and before a recess, at question time and, if any succeed in catching the Speakers' eye, in the course of general debate.

However, many Members of Parliament soon discover that their opportunities to contribute significantly to debate are few. All such debates are limited by the political framework in which they are held and individual members have no means of probing behind the statements of Ministers seeking to justify departmental decisions. The influence of the member on government policy from the backbenches or in opposition is also negligible, and it often seems that the conduct of public administration cannot be effectively scrutinised by the House of Commons. It has been said that any effective participation of backbench Members of Parliament in decision making will continue to present very great difficulties as long as governments maintain majorities in the House with the aid of an electoral system under which the winner can expect to take almost all, and as long as constitutional rules leave the spending power entirely in the hands of the Executive.

It is these limitations that have given rise to demands for other procedures by which the House may inform and concern itself more directly with the work of government. In this respect experience has shown that it is possible within the existing British parliamentary system for members to influence the conduct of administration and to modify aspects of policy by their scrutiny of administrative activity as members of select committees. Indeed many people have seen in the increased use of select committees the key to a more effective role for Parliament vis-a-vis government. Between 1967 and 1978 these committees did offer some detailed and imaginative suggestions for administrative reorganisation, and made themselves, the House in general and interested members of the public better informed about central administration and the views of the administration.

However, it was not until 1979 that a bold experiment to extend the opportunity for members to scrutinise the Executive through specialised select committees was started. Twelve select committees were established to monitor the activities of particular government departments or groups of departments. Their terms of reference were to examine the expenditure, administration and policy of the principal government departments, with the power to send for papers and witnesses and to appoint sub-committees. The committees also have the power to appoint technical advisors to supply information which is not readily available or to elucidate matters of complexity.

But while their investigation and reports show that they are effective in putting pressure on the government, there are limitations. No sanctions exist in respect of ministers who refuse to appear. There is still no guaranteed time for debating their reports. Also the Party Whips effectively choose the members of their party who are to serve on a particular committee. This enables the Party Frontbench to exclude from a committee any member who is likely to oppose frontbench policy. Thus the government will attempt to exclude from a committee members of its own party who are likely to join with the opposition to produce a report critical of the government.

Nevertheless, reports critical of the government are produced, but this 'packing' of committees by the Party Whips clearly reduces the potential effectiveness of select committees as a device for exercising control over the government. A further step towards increasing the effectiveness of members over government policy, this time in the field of national expenditure, has been the enactment of the National Audit Act 1983. The Act provides for the Comptroller and Auditor General to become an officer of Parliament and to head a National Audit Office. A Public Accounts Commission is also established consisting of the Chairman of the Public Accounts Committee, the Leader of the House and seven other MPs who are not Ministers of State. This has vastly increased parliamentary control over national expenditure.

Therefore the ineffectual role of so many backbenchers may be a serious weakness of the House of Commons. But while the role of the backbencher in the Chamber itself may be ineffectual, opportunities do exist through the select committee system for his full participation in serious and effective scrutiny of government policy and administration.

QUESTION 3

Critically assess the statement that Parliament legitimates but does not legislate.

University of London LLB Examination
(for External Students) Constitutional Law June 1983 Q4

General comment

This question requires discussion of the idea of a separation of powers in the British parliamentary system. You need to write an introduction explaining the basic principles of separation of power and then decide if, as between the Executive and Legislature, it exists in this country. Does the Executive control the Legislature or vice versa? Remember the statement does not mention the independence of the Judiciary - so you in answering should also not really discuss it. We are concerned only with Executive/Legislature relations.

Skeleton solution

* The doctrine of the separation of powers with the example of the USA which is based on the theory.

* The evolution of Cabinet government in the UK with particular reference to government dominance in the Commons.

* The nature of the relationship between Parliament and the government with reference to parliamentary controls on government.

Suggested solution

The doctrine of the separation of powers has taken several forms at different periods and in different contexts. Aristotle is probably its first exponent, followed much later by John Locke in his second treatise of Civil Government in 1690, and then given a more popular treatment by Montesquieu in the eighteenth century. John Locke simply reasoned that as power corrupts men 'The three organs of state must not get into one hand'. Montesquieu developed the theory basing his analysis on a idealised picture of the British Constitution in 1700s. He decided that there are three main classes of government function: the legislative, the executive and the judicial and that these should be exercised by three main organs of government - the Legislature, the Executive and the Judiciary. He felt that to concentrate more than one class of function in any one person or organ of government is a threat to individual liberty. For example the Executive should not be allowed to make laws, or adjudicate on alleged breaches of the law and it should be concerned only with the making and applying of policy and general administration.

The best modern model of the doctrine is in the United States. The President and his 'Cabinet', the Executive, cannot be members of Congress, the Legislature. The Judiciary can declare legislation void, however this has in reality produced judges who are political appointments. The doctrine is embodied in the Constitution. In contrast no one would claim that the separation of powers is a central feature of the modern British Constitution.

Since the evolution of the Cabinet system with the Ministers of the Crown exercising executive power, and also sitting in Parliament the legislative body, there has been a direct link between Executive and Legislature power. In a sense the statement in question is true, but to see how true it is, a closer examination of the system is needed.

By convention Ministers of the Crown who form the Cabinet should be members of one or other House of Parliament. However since the House of Commons Disqualification Act 1975 the maximum number of ministers in the Commons is 95. Except for these ministers, under the same statute, the vast majority of persons who hold positions within the Executive are disqualified from membership of the Commons, namely all members of the civil service, armed forces, police and holders of many other public offices. It is only really the Ministers who form part of the Legislature and the Executive.

The statement in essence is suggesting that the Executive controls the Legislature. Ultimately this is untrue as Parliament can oust a government it does not like by withdrawing support. However this system of electoral representation together with the use of Whips makes such a reversal highly unlikely. A government usually is returned with an overall majority in the House of Commons and has virtual control over Parliament. The government will have a majority on all House of Commons committees. The Whips ensure that the party line is not broken and also that a majority can be summoned at short notice to vote in the Commons. Devices such as the guillotine are used to curtail parliamentary debate of legislation. A government such as the one returned in 1986 under Mrs Margaret Thatcher with a large majority should have little trouble in pushing through legislation built to implement the Tory policies. In substance the Government does seem to make law.

It is possible to argue that the Legislature is not merely a 'rubber stamp' and that it controls the government through Ministers' Question Time, Adjournment Debates, select committees, Opposition Days and just general opposition to the Executive policy. It is true to say that probing questions can disturb the path of government policy. A recent example may be the Local Government Finance Act 1988. Matters of great public concern can usually be at the very least delayed by the Legislature.

The Executive also produces a great number of statutory instruments which are a form of delegated legislation and not questioned in the Commons. This usually is to deal with details within the Minister's domain (eg Planning for the Secretary of State for the Environment) but it is in theory a powerful example of the Executive exercising the functions of the legislature. In conclusion it is true to say that on most occasions Parliament merely legitimates the actions of the Executive but this blending of Executive and Legislature is a fundamental characteristic of the British system of government. It existed to a lesser extent in Montesquieu's day and with the growth of Cabinet and Prime Ministerial government it has grown too - any attempt to change it would produce startling results for our unwritten Constitution.

7   LEGISLATURE II - THE HOUSE OF LORDS

7.1 Introduction

7.2 Key points

7.3 Recent cases and statutes

7.4 Analysis of questions

7.5 Questions

7.1   Introduction

The House of Lords is a non-elected chamber. It plays a part in the legislative process but ultimately its powers are very limited. Nevertheless many argue that the quality of debate in the House of Lords is high and the House can sometimes effectively challenge the Commons.

The reform/abolition of the House of Lords has been on the political agenda for many years but other than the Life Peerages Act 1958 which has very much re-vitalised the House no significant attempts at reform have been successful.

7.2   Key points

a) *The composition of the House of Lords*

   i) The Lords Spiritual: Archbishops of Canterbury and York, the Bishops of London, Durham and Winchester, and the next 21 diocesan bishops of the Church of England in seniority of appointment.

   ii) The Lords Temporal:

   • Hereditary peers and peeresses in their own right of England, Scotland, Great Britain and the United Kingdom.

   • Life peers created under the Life Peerages Act 1958.

   • Lords of Appeal in Ordinary.

b) *The functions and work of the House of Lords*

   The 1968 Government White Paper *House of Lords Reform* referred to seven functions of the House of Lords.

   i) Its appellate role as the supreme court of appeal.

   ii) The provision of a forum for free debate and matters of public interest.

   iii) The revision of Public Bills brought from the House of Commons.

   iv) The initiation of Public Bills.

   v) The consideration of subordinate legislation.

vi) The scrutiny of the activities of the Executive.

vii) The scrutiny of private legislation.

c)   *House of Lords reform*

i)   The Parliament Act 1911

• A Bill certified by the Speaker as a Money Bill should receive the Royal Assent and become an Act of Parliament without the consent of the House of Lords if, having been sent up from the House of Commons at least one month before the end of the session, it had not been passed by the Lords without amendment within one month of its being sent up.

• Any other Public Bill, except one for extending the life of Parliament, could become an Act of Parliament without the consent of the House of Lords if it had been passed by the House of Commons in three successive sessions, two years having elapsed between its Second Reading and its final passing in the House of Commons, and if it had been sent up to the House of Lords at least one month before the end of each of the three sessions.

• The maximum duration of a Parliament was reduced from seven years to five.

ii)   The Parliament Act 1949

• Amends the Parliament Act 1911 by reducing the number of sessions in which a Bill must be passed by the House of Commons from three to two, and reducing the period between the Second Reading and final passing in the House of Commons from two years to one.

iii)   The Peerage Act 1963

• This Act enables hereditary peers, other than those of first creation, to renounce their titles for life by disclaimer. The peerage remains dormant and devolves upon the heir in the normal manner on the renouncer's death. A person who has disclaimed a peerage is entitled to vote in Parliamentary elections and is eligible for election to the House of Commons.

iv)   The Parliament (No 2) Bill 1969

In November 1968 the Labour Government published a White Paper, *House of Lords Reform*, which was later embodied in the Parliament (No 2) Bill 1968-69. Its main proposals were as follows:

• The reformed House of Lords was to be a two-tier structure comprising voting peers and non-voting peers.

• Succession to a hereditary peerage was no longer to carry the right to a seat in the House of Lords, but existing peers by succession would have the right to sit as non-voting members during their life time, or might be created life peers to enable them to continue in active participation as voting members.

- Voting peers were expected to play a full part in the work of the House and be required to attend at least one-third of the sittings. They would be subject to an age of retirement. Non-voting peers would be able to play a full part in debates and in committees, but would not be entitled to vote.

- The voting House would initially consist of about 230 peers, distributed between the parties in such a way as to give the government a small majority over the Opposition parties, but not a majority of the House as a whole when those without party allegiance were included.

- The reformed House would be able to impose a delay of six months from the date of disagreement between the two Houses on the passage of non-financial public legislation. After this delay a Bill could be submitted for Royal Assent by resolution of the House of Commons.

- The Lords would be able to require the House of Commons to reconsider subordinate legislation, but would not be able to reject it outright.

- A review would be made of the functions and procedures of the two Houses once the main reform had come into effect.

The Bill was abandoned on April 17, 1969.

7.3   Recent cases and statutes

As with the House of Commons students need to consider the many recent political issues, usually controversial, that have involved the House of Lords. Examples here could indicate the effectiveness or otherwise of the House in exercising its role within the Constitution.

Local Government Finance Act 1988

Education Act 1988

7.4   Analysis of questions

The House of Lords is a popular topic for examiners. Questions demand a knowledge of the role and function of the House and may in addition require the student to consider the relationship between the House of Commons and the House of Lords or the implications of reform of the House of Lords. The tendency to write in a highly descriptive way everything known about the topic must be resisted.

7.5   Questions

QUESTION 1

'While a second chamber is needed to serve a number of legislative purposes the present House of Lords is restricted by its composition from exercising its powers effectively.' (Wade and Bradley).

Discuss.

University of London LLB Examination
(for External Students) Constitutional Law June 1986 Q4

General comment

The usual House of Lords question. As always don't write everything you know about the House of Lords and don't be tempted to simply turn out the traditional (and now largely discredited) criticisms of the Lords. Remember that while the undemocratic nature of its composition is a major criticism of the House, it is also one of its greatest assets.

Skeleton solution

- Introduction; the need for a second chamber.

- The criticisms of the hereditary and life peerage systems.

- The advantages which flow from the undemocratic nature of the composition of the House of Lords.

- The factors limiting the effective exercise of the powers of the House.

Suggested solution

For many years there has been opposition to the continued existence of the House of Lords as the second chamber in our present bicameral parliamentary system. Nevertheless the fact remains that a second chamber is needed to assist in the legislative process and the House of Lords performs the functions of a second chamber extremely well.

However, despite the success of the House of Lords in performing its functions it can be argued that the House is nevertheless restricted by its aristocratic and unrepresentative composition from exercising its powers effectively. In a democracy, it may be argued all legislators should be directly accountable to the people at elections or at least accountable indirectly, for example, by election by the House of Commons. Their Lordships, however, take their seats in the legislature either because they are hereditary peers or because they have been created life peers under the Life Peerages Act 1958. The former are criticised on the grounds that high office should be awarded to those who earn it on merit and not by accident of birth, and as most hereditary peers are Conservative this leads to a permanent Conservative majority in the House. The life peers are criticised because of the considerable powers of patronage left in the hands of the Prime Minister to reward party loyalists and retiring ministers with seats in the Upper Chamber. It is also thought by some that since the members of the House of Lords do not represent any body of constituents they speak for a small privileged section of the community.

But criticism of the composition of the House of Lords is often ill-founded and uninformed. It can be argued that the composition of the House does not directly affect the effectiveness of the chamber - quite the opposite. The quality of members and speeches is often very high. Debates are well informed. Those upon whom peerages are conferred are usually persons with considerable experience of politics, public service or industry, or who have otherwise made their mark in public or intellectual life. They bring to the House a wide range of expertise. The hereditary element also provides many young peers and because the Lords do not have any constituencies to consider they can devote more time to their parliamentary duties and do not have to worry about re-selection or re-election. In many respects therefore the membership of the House of Lords is far superior to that of the House of Commons. The only difficulty is the undemocratic nature of their appointment.

It is the consciousness of their undemocratic nature of appointment which is the major impediment to the effectiveness of the House. While the 1911 and 1949 Parliament Acts did have a direct effect on the effectiveness of the House of Lords - for example, the House no longer has power over money matters and governments no longer depend on the favour of the Lords for their continuation in office - nevertheless under the Parliament Acts their Lordships do retain the power to amend non-money Bills. Although the House of Lords cannot impose its will on the Commons in legislation, it can effectively delay Government Bills for one year. But the Lords are reluctant to exercise their suspensory powers over legislation which they still retain. If they interfere with government business they may lay themselves open to allegations of seeking to frustrate the wishes of the people as expressed through their democratically elected government.

This makes the House of Lords extremely vulnerable. How can they act as a check on the House of Commons in such circumstances? The Government can brush aside opposition in the House of Lords 'because they don't represent the people', and the threat of abolition or reform is always present. Their Lordships are well aware of this. This is perhaps one reason why in spite of their inbuilt Conservative majority they have always shown restraint when dealing with Labour government legislation. Recent events have shown however that the reports of the impotence of the House of Lords have been exaggerated and that, given the right circumstances, its effectiveness and efficiency is not altogether impaired by these legislative and political constraints.

When the threat of abolition is lifted, as it usually is under a Conservative Government, their Lordships can be very effective in carrying out their constitutional functions. The Lords retain a high degree of political independence inherent in their undemocratic character. They do not have to rely upon the continued support of a political party for their seats in the legislature and while the majority of hereditary peers may be Conservative, a Conservative Government is not guaranteed a majority in the House. They vote according to their conscience, not the demands of the Whips. Where the government has a heavy legislative programme, amendment or delay in the Lords can seriously threaten the legislative timetable for that particular session and the government will be forced to take notice and attempt a compromise with the Lords. If compromise fails and the government implements the procedure under the Parliament Acts, even a one year delay may prove fatal to the government's plans.

But such opposition is possible only where the House of Lords retains popular support for its action, where, for example, the government is acting unconstitutionally or outside the terms of its mandate, or as in the present parliamentary situation where the government majority in the House of Commons is such that there is no effective and efficient opposition in the Commons. In other situations their Lordships may be reluctant to seriously oppose the government's wishes. The fear of abolition or public censure would be decisive.

Therefore while the effectiveness of the House of Lords in respect of its legislative functions and powers is relatively unimpeded and in many respects enhanced by the anachronistic and undemocratic nature of its composition, its effectiveness as a check upon the House of Commons, and thus in reality upon the government of the day, is limited.

QUESTION 2

Outline the constitutional problems and benefits, if any, that would arise if the House of Lords were abolished.

University of London LLB Examination
(for External Students) Constitutional Law June 1985 Q3

General comment

This question involves discussion of the role of the House of Lords as the second chamber in our bicameral parliamentary system and the constitutional problems and benefits which would arise if the Lords were abolished in favour of an unicameral parliamentary system. Don't write everything you know about the House of Lords and don't be tempted to simply turn out the traditional (and now largely discredited) criticisms of Lords as justification for their abolition. Remember, the House of Lords plays a vital function as a revision chamber and helps relieve the pressure of work on the already overburdened House of Commons. Events in recent years have also shown that the House of Lords is the only effective check on a Government which dominates the House of Commons. It is doubtful whether any real benefits would arise from the abolition of the House of Lords. Reform yes, abolition no.

Skeleton solution

* Introduction: arguments for reform/abolition of the House of Lords.

* The problems caused by adopting a unicameral parliamentary system. The position of the Judicial Committee; role of the House as a revision chamber for Public Bills; inability of Commons to deal adequately with all Bills passed; need for fundamental change in House of Commons procedure; role of Lords as a check on the Executive; need for written Constitution/Bill of Rights.

* Benefits of abolition: saving of costs; space; forcing of change and reform of House of Commons procedures.

Suggested solution

For many years there has been opposition of some sort or another to the continued existence of the House of Lords as the second chamber in our present bicameral parliamentary system. The argument is that as presently constituted the House of Lords is undemocratic, outdated and unsuitable in a modern society. Some therefore favour reform, so that, for example, its composition becomes more democratic and its powers perhaps increased so that it can act as a more effective check on the House of Commons, (and thus, in reality, on the government of the day), than it does at present. Others, however, wish to go further still and see the total abolition of the second chamber altogether in favour of a unicameral parliamentary system.

If the House of Lords were abolished in favour of a unicameral parliamentary system certain constitutional problems would undoubtedly result. Whether these problems would be insuperable is a matter of opinion. What cannot be denied, however, is that despite the problems regarding its composition, the fact remains that the House of Lords does perform a valuable service within the present parliamentary system and if abolished many of its functions would still have to be performed by some other body, presumably the House of Commons. In 1968, the Government White Paper *House of Lords Reform* referred to seven functions of the House of Lords. An examination of each of these functions serves to illustrate some of the problems that might result from abolition.

Firstly, the House of Lords acts as the final court of appeal for the whole of the United Kingdom in civil cases and for England, Wales and Northern Ireland in criminal cases. If the House were abolished therefore a new 'supreme' court would have to be established to take its place, unless of course the Court of Appeal were to become the final appeal court for England and Wales. However, as the judicial work of the House is separate from its other functions and only involves the Judicial Committee - drawn from the Lord High Chancellor, the Lords of Appeal in Ordinary and Lords who hold or have held high judicial office - the separation of the Judicial Committee from the rest of the House of Lords or its replacement by some new body would not perhaps cause too great a constitutional problem.

Secondly, the House provides a forum for free debate on matters of public interest, Wednesday in particular being traditionally set aside for special debate on a wide range of subjects. Apart from the fact that these debates are usually of a very high standard; a standard that would perhaps never be reached in the Commons, even if the time were available, this loss would not pose any great constitutional problem.

Thirdly, and perhaps most importantly, the House acts as a revising chamber for Public Bills brought from the House of Commons. About one half of the time of the House of Lords is devoted to the consideration of Public Bills. The majority of this time is spent on revising Bills which have already passed the Commons, where the great majority of government legislation is introduced. The House of Commons does not have the time to fully debate all the legislation it has to pass each session and the use of procedures for the curtailment of debate, such as the guillotine, often means that Bills are passed by the Commons without really being considered at all. A second chamber is therefore required to examine and revise such Bills. If the second chamber is abolished then the procedures of the House of Commons for enacting legislation will have to be changed if the present standard and volume of legislation is to be maintained. This could be achieved by Membership of the House of Commons becoming full-time and by making even more use of committees. However, even then the volume of legislation may still prove to be too great, necessitating either a shortening of the procedure by which a Bill is enacted or making more use of subordinate legislation, which some would argue is already over used as it is. Certainly some fundamental changes would have to be made to the proceedings of the House of Commons and these may prove unacceptable to many of the present MPs.

Also it must be remembered that the House of Commons, because of the distortion produced by our electoral system, is largely controlled by a government which does not represent even 50 per cent of the electorate. A second chamber is thus required to at least delay substantially controversial legislation which may be unpopular with the majority of the people of the country. If the second chamber is abolished then the only way to control a government with an absolute majority in the House of Commons may be to have either a written Constitution or a Bill of Rights containing entrenched clauses, perhaps requiring a referendum for amendment.

The House of Lords also initiates Public Bills. While the more important and controversial Bills almost invariably begin in the House of Commons, Bills which are relatively uncontroversial in party political terms are regularly introduced in the House of Lords. If abolished, these Bills will have to be dealt with by the Commons thus adding to its already overburdened workload. Similarly, the subordinate legislation and the private legislation at present dealt with by the House of Lords would also fall to be wholly dealt with by the Commons if the second chamber were abolished.

The arguments in favour of a unicameral Parliament are mainly political and it is doubtful whether any real practical benefit would result from the abolition of the House of Lords. Certainly it is doubtful that the loss of the Lords could ever be compensated for. However, there are benefits of sorts which would flow from abolition, such as the saving of money and the making available of more space in the Palace of Westminster. Abolition would also have to result in the widespread reform of the House of Commons if any semblance of a parliamentary democracy is to be maintained. Such reform may be viewed as a substantial benefit. However, the main fear, and indeed the most likely consequence of the abolition of the House of Lords, is that it will simply serve to strengthen the Executive control of the Legislature.

QUESTION 3

What contribution, if any, does the House of Lords make to the British Constitution?

University of London LLB Examination
(for External Students) Constitutional Law June 1987 Q4

General comment

Another typical House of Lords question. The question involves discussion of the role of the House of Lords as the second chamber in our bicameral parliamentary system and the effects to the Constitution which would arise if the Lords were not there.

Skeleton solution

•   Introduction. General position of the House of Lords within the Constitution.

•   The role of the House of Lords. The work of the Judicial Committee; role of the House as a revision chamber for Public Bills; role of Lords as a check on the Executive.

- Effects on the British Constitution if the House of Lords abolished. Need for change in House of Commons procedure; need for written Constitution.

Suggested solution

The House of Lords is the second chamber in our bicameral parliamentary system. To its critics, the House of Lords as presently constituted is undemocratic, out-dated and unsuitable in a modern society. Many therefore favour reform, so that for example its composition becomes more democratic. Others, however, wish to go further still and see the total abolition of the House of Lords. But those in favour of abolition fail to realise that the House of Lords makes a valuable contribution to the British Constitution. Despite the problems regarding its composition, the fact remains that the House of Lords does perform a valuable service within the present parliamentary system and if abolished many of its functions would still have to be performed by some other body, presumably the House of Commons. In 1968, the Government White Paper *House of Lords Reform* referred to seven functions of the House of Lords. An examination of each of these functions serves to illustrate the contribution made by the House to the effective working of our Constitution and highlight some of the problems that might result if the House of Lords ceased to exist.

Firstly, the House of Lords acts as the final court of appeal for the whole of the United Kingdom in civil cases and for England, Wales and Northern Ireland in criminal cases. The judicial work of the House is separate from its other functions and only involves the Judicial Committee, drawn from the Lord High Chancellor, the Lords of Appeal in Ordinary and Lords who hold or who have held high judicial office. Nevertheless it is extremely valuable to have the senior judiciary present in the legislature and able to contribute during the passing of Bills. Of course, if the House of Lords did not exist a new 'supreme court' would have to be established to take its place, unless of course the Court of Appeal were to become the final appeal court for England and Wales.

Secondly, the House of Lords provides a forum for free debate on matters of public interest, Wednesday in particular being traditionally set aside for special debate on a wide range of subjects. Apart from the fact that these debates are usually of a very high standard, a standard that would perhaps never be reached in the Commons, even if the time were available, their loss would not pose any great constitutional problem.

Thirdly, and perhaps most importantly, the House acts as a revising chamber for Public Bills brought from the House of Commons. About one half of the time of the House of Lords is devoted to the consideration of Public Bills. The majority of this time is spent on revising Bills which have already passed the Commons, where the great majority of government legislation is introduced. The House of Commons does not have the time to fully debate all the legislation it has to pass each session and the use of procedures for the curtailment of debate, such as the guillotine, often means that Bills are passed by the Commons without really being considered at all. A second chamber is therefore required to examine and revise such Bills. This is the greatest contribution made by the House of Lords to the British Constitution and it is probably true to say that as far as this particular function is concerned, if the House of

Lords did not exist then it would have to be invented. If the House ceased to exist then the procedures of the House of Commons for enacting legislation would have to be changed if the present standard and volume of legislation were to be maintained. This could be achieved by membership of the House of Commons becoming full-time and by making even more use of committees. However, even then the volume of legislation may still prove to be too great, necessitating either a shortening of the procedure by which a Bill is enacted or making more use of subordinate legislation, which some would argue is already over used as it is.

Certainly some fundamental changes would have to be made to the procedures of the House of Commons. Also it must be remembered that the House of Commons, because of the distortion produced by our electoral system, is largely controlled by a government which does not represent even 50 per cent of the electorate. A second chamber is thus required to at least delay substantially controversial legislation which may be unpopular with the majority of the people of the country. If the House of Lords were not there then the only way to control a government with an absolute majority in the House of Commons may be to have either a written Constitution or a Bill of Rights containing entrenched clauses, perhaps requiring a referendum for amendment. Experience has shown that the House of Lords, with its independent membership, is the only check that exists on the present Conservative government and frequent defeats have been inflicted by their Lordships, thus helping to weaken executive control of the legislature.

The House of Lords also initiates Public Bills. While the more controversial and important Bills almost invariably begin in the House of Commons, Bills which are relatively uncontroversial in party political terms are regularly introduced in the House of Lords. If the House did not exist these Bills would have to be dealt with by the Commons thus adding to its already overburdened workload. Similarly; the subordinate legislation and the private legislation at present dealt with by the House of Lords would also fall to be wholly dealt with by the Commons if the second chamber did not exist.

It can be seen therefore that the House of Lords makes a very great contribution to the effective and efficient working of the British Constitution.

QUESTION 4

The House of Lords as at present constituted is a useful legislative chamber but several factors impair its efficiency.

Discuss.

University of London LLB Examination
(for External Students) Constitutional Law June 1984 Q4

General comment

This particular question involves discussion of the factors impairing the efficiency of the House of Lords as a legislative chamber. Remember that recent events have shown that the House of Lords is doing its job rather well and is the only effective check on the Conservative government which dominates the House of Commons. So don't fall into the trap of simply turning out the traditional criticism and dismissing the Lords as out of date, undemocratic, aristocratic and impotent. Events have shown that in spite of the Parliament Act and the threat of abolition it is as efficient and effective as ever in doing its job as a legislative chamber if it has the will and popular support to do so.

Skeleton solution

• Introduction outlining function to the House of Lords.

• Composition of the House of Lords - Life Peerage Act 1958.

• Factors impairing efficiency: composition undemocratic; Acts of 1911 and 1949; lack of public confidence undermines challenges to government.

Suggested solution

The House of Lords as at present constituted is indeed a useful legislative chamber. Many of the less controversial Government Bills are introduced there thus allowing the Government's legislative output to be increased and its efficiency improved. Several Private Members' Bills have also been successfully introduced in the Lords after having been crowded out in the Commons, and the House performs a useful function as a forum for the consideration of private Bills. The House of Lords also performs extremely well the important function of revising Commons' Bills, acting as a revising chamber correcting the errors which are bound to occur in the drafting of the numerous Bills each government introduces in every parliamentary session.

However, despite the success of the House of Lords in performing their functions, several factors do impair the efficiency of the Chamber. The major problems stem from the composition of the House. Many argue that the House of Lords is not at present well fitted to carry out its functions because of its aristocratic and unrepresentative membership. In a democracy, they argue, all legislators should be directly accountable to the people at elections or at least accountable indirectly, for example, by election by the House of Commons. Their Lordships, however, take their seats in the legislature either because they are hereditary peers or because they have been created life peers under the Life Peerages Act 1958. The former are criticised on the grounds that high office should be awarded to those who earn it on merit and not by accident of birth, and as most hereditary peers are Conservative this leads to a permanent Conservative majority in the House. The life peers are criticised because of the considerable powers of patronage left in the hands of the Prime Minister to reward party loyalists and retiring Ministers with seats in the Upper Chamber. It is also thought by some that since the members of the House of Lords do not represent any body of constituents they speak for a small privileged section of the community.

But criticism of the membership of the House of Lords is often ill-founded and uninformed. It can be argued that the composition of the House does not directly affect the efficiency of the Chamber - quite the opposite. The quality of members and speeches is often very high. Debates are well informed. Those upon whom peerages are conferred are usually persons with considerable experience of politics, public service or industry, or who have otherwise made their mark in public or intellectual life. They bring to the House a wide range of expertise. The hereditary element also provides many young peers and because the Lords do not have any constituencies to consider they can devote more time to their parliamentary duties and don't have to worry about re-selection or re-election. In many respects, therefore, the membership of the House of Lords is far superior to that of the House of Commons. The only difficulty is the undemocratic nature of their appointment.

It is the consciousness of their undemocratic nature of appointment which is the major impediment to the efficiency of the House. The 1911 and 1949 Parliament Acts did have a direct effect on the efficiency of the House of Lords. The House no longer has power over money matters and governments no longer depend on the favour of the Lords for their continuation in office. But, under the Parliament Acts their Lordships do retain the power to amend non-money Bills and although the House cannot impose its will on the Commons in legislation, it can effectively delay Government Bills for one year. But the Lords are reluctant to exercise their suspensory powers over legislation which they still retain. If they interfere with government business they lay themselves open to allegations of seeking to frustrate the wishes of the people as expressed through their democratically elected government.

This makes the House of Lords extremely vulnerable. How can they act as a check on the House of Commons in such circumstances? The Government can brush aside opposition in the House of Lords 'because they don't represent the people', and the threat of abolition or reform is always present. Their Lordships are well aware of this. This is perhaps one reason why in spite of their supposed inbuilt Conservative majority they have always shown restraint when dealing with Labour government legislation. Recent events, however, have shown that the reports of the impotence of the House of Lords have been exaggerated and that given the right circumstances its effectiveness and efficiency is not altogether impaired by these legislative and political constraints.

When the threat of abolition is lifted, as it usually is under a Conservative government, their Lordships can be very effective in carrying out their constitutional functions. The Lords retain a high degree of political independence inherent in their undemocratic character. They do not have to rely upon the constituted support of a political party for their seats in the legislature and while the majority of hereditary peers may be Conservative, a Conservative government is not guaranteed a majority in the House. They vote according to their conscience, not the demands of the Whips. Where the government has a heavy legislative programme amendment or delay in the Lords can seriously threaten the legislative timetable for that particular session and the government will be forced to take notice and attempt a compromise with the Lords. If compromise fails and the government implements the procedure under the Parliament Acts, even a one year delay may prove fatal to the government's plans.

But such opposition is only possible where the House of Lords retains popular support for its action, where, for example, the government is acting unconstitutionally or outside the terms of its mandate, or as in the present parliamentary situation where the government majority in the House of Commons is such that there is no effective and efficient opposition in the Commons. In other situations their Lordships may be reluctant to seriously oppose the government's wishes. The fear of abolition or public censure would be decisive.

Therefore while the efficiency of the House of Lords in respect of its legislative functions is relatively unimpeded and in many respects enhanced by its anachronistic and undemocratic features, its effectiveness as a check upon the House of Commons may in some situations be seriously affected by a lack of political confidence resulting from the undemocratic nature of its composition.

8   PARLIAMENTARY PRIVILEGE

8.1   Introduction

8.2   Key points

8.3   Recent cases and statutes

8.4   Analysis of questions

8.5   Questions

8.1   Introduction

For a Member of Parliament to carry out his duties to his constituents properly he must be free to raise matters without the fear of being sued for slander or libel. Parliamentary privilege allows him to do so within the confines of Parliament itself. There is, of course, the risk of abuse and, in any event, the counter argument that those attacked may not have a chance to defend themselves.

It is sometimes said that the rules of parliamentary privilege constitute a clear case of 'power without responsibility', but it has to be accepted that over the years parliamentary privilege has been essential to the exposure of injustices and malpractices which the restrictive English libel laws might otherwise have allowed to continue unchecked.

As with most of constitutional law it is a matter of striking the right balance; in this area the need for freedom of speech in Parliament has to be respected and, perhaps, all that needs to be changed to achieve the balance is for Parliament itself to be much more willing to impose heavy penalties on those Members who are deemed to have abused this privilege.

8.2   Key points

It is important that students understand the following issues regarding parliamentary privilege:

a)   *Definition*

Parliamentary privilege is defined by Erskine May in *Parliamentary Practice*, 18th edition) as:

' ... the sum of the peculiar rights enjoyed by each House collectively as a constitutional part of the High Court of Parliament and by members of each House individually, without which they could not discharge their functions, and which exceed those possessed by other bodies or individuals.'

b)   *Privileges of the House of Commons*

i)   'Ancient and undoubted rights and privileges'

At the opening of each Parliament, the Speaker formally claims from the Crown for the Commons 'their ancient and undoubted rights and privileges'. These are:

- Freedom of Speech in Debate

    The right is guaranteed in Article 9 of the Bill of Rights 1689 which provides:

    'the freedom of speech and debates or proceedings in Parliament ought not to be impeached or questioned in any court or place out of Parliament.'

    No Member may be made liable in the courts for words spoken in the course of parliamentary proceedings.

    What is said in Parliament cannot be used to support a cause of action in defamation which has arisen outside Parliament: *Church of Scientology* v *Johnson-Smith* [1972] 1 QB 522.

    What are proceedings in Parliament? Remarks made in debate, discussions in committee, parliamentary questions and answers, and votes are clearly within the definition. Other words spoken within the precincts of Parliament unconnected with parliamentary proceedings are not protected: *Rivlin* v *Bilainkin* [1953] 1 QB 485.

    As indicated in section 8.4 Analysis of questions, a likely point for consideration in the examination question is what is 'a proceeding in Parliament'. In this regard it should be noted that this may cover matters said outside the parliamentary chamber. Students should note the following statement from Viscount Radcliffe in *Attorney-General for Ceylon* v *De Livera* [1963] AC 103 in which he was considering what was meant by a proceeding in Parliament:

    'the answer given to that somewhat more limited question depends upon the following consideration, in what circumstances and in what situations is a member of the House exercising his "real" or "essential" function as a member ... the most that can be said is that, despite reluctance to treat a member's privileges as going beyond anything that is essential, it is generally recognised that it is impossible to regard his only proper functions as a member as being confined to what he does on the floor of the House.'

    Particular problems have frequently arisen regarding the status of communications between MPs and Ministers: *Case of GWR Strauss MP* (1957-58). Such communications may only enjoy qualified privilege under the law of defamation: *Beach* v *Freeson* [1972] QB 14.

    Letters from members of the public to MPs enjoy only qualified privilege under the law of defamation: *R* v *Rule* [1937] 2 KB 375.

Communications between MPs and the Parliamentary Commissioner for Administration are accorded absolute privilege in the law of defamation: Parliamentary Commissioners Act 1967, s10(5).

The fair and accurate reporting of parliamentary proceedings is protected by qualified privilege at common law: *Wason* v *Walter* (1869) LR 4 QB 73; *Cook* v *Alexander* [1974] QB 279.

Fair and accurate extracts from, or abstracts of, papers published under the authority of Parliament enjoy qualified privilege in the law of defamation: Parliamentary Papers Act 1840.

* Freedom from arrest

    The immunity only applies to civil arrest and extends while Parliament sits and for 40 days before and 40 days after: *Stourton* v *Stourton* [1963] P 302.

    The immunity does not protect Members from arrest on criminal charges.

* Freedom of access to Her Majesty whenever occasion shall require; and that the most favourable construction should be placed upon all their proceedings.

ii) Other privileges

The other privileges of the House of Commons, not expressly claimed by the Speaker include:

* The right of the House to regulate its own composition

    The House retains the exclusive right to determine by resolution when a writ for the holding of a by-election shall be issued.

    The House maintains the right to determine whether a Member is qualified to sit in the House and can declare a Member's seat vacant on grounds of legal disqualification or for any other reason it thinks fit.

    The House may expel a Member whom it considers unfit to sit: the *case of Gary Allingham MP* (1947).

* The right to take exclusive cognisance of matters arising within the precincts of the House

    The House maintains the right to control its own proceedings and regulate its internal affairs without interference from the courts: *Bradlaugh* v *Gossett* (1884) 12 QBD 271.

    If a statute is to bind the House it must do so clearly: *R* v *Graham-Campbell ex parte Herbert* [1935] 1 KB 594.

iii) The right to punish both Members and non-members for breach of privilege and contempt

The House has the power to maintain its privileges and to punish those who break or commit contempt of the House.

Contempt of the House is a very wide concept. Erskine May describes it as:

' ... any act or omission which obstructs or impedes either House or Parliament in the performance of its functions, or which obstructs or impedes any member or officer of such House in the discharge of his duty, or which has a tendency, directly or indirectly, to produce such results may be treated as a contempt even though there is no precedent of the offence.'

Thus while the House cannot create new privileges, except by statute, there is no complete list of behaviour which constitutes contempt.

Complaints of breach of privilege may be raised by a Member or in the House by the Speaker. If the Speaker rules that a prima facie case has been made out a motion is proposed that the matter be referred to the Committee of Privileges.

The Committee of Privileges comprises the 15 most senior Members of the House. It is the master of its own proceedings. It can compel the attendance of witnesses and the production of documents; failure to comply being a contempt. There is no requirement of legal representation.

The Select Committee on Parliamentary Privilege in 1967 recommended that persons directly concerned in the Committee's investigations should have the right to attend its hearings, make submissions, call, examine and cross-examine witnesses, and be legally represented and apply for legal aid.

Offenders may be reprimanded or admonished or committed to prison. Members may be suspended or expelled from the House.

iv) The right of impeachment (now obsolete)

c) *The courts and parliamentary privilege*

The House of Commons claims to be the absolute and sole judge of its own privileges and maintains that its judgment cannot be called into question by any other court. The courts do not agree. They maintain the right to determine the nature and extent of parliamentary privilege when adjudicating upon the rights of individuals outside the house. This disagreement has given rise to constitutional conflict: *Stockdale* v *Hansard* (1839) 9 Ad & E 1; *Case of the Sheriffs of Middlesex* (1840) Ad & E 273.

d) *MPs as representatives of outside interests*

If a Member agrees to represent an outside interest group in Parliament, is a threat by that group to remove support from the Member a breach of privilege?

i) It is improper for a Member to enter into any arrangement fettering his complete independence by undertaking to press some particular point of view on behalf of an outside interest whether for reward or not: *case of WJ Brown MP* (1947).

ii) It is improper to attempt to punish a Member financially because of his actions as a Member: *Case of the Yorkshire Area Council of National Union of Mineworkers* (1975).

e) *Privileges of the House of Lords*

The privileges of the House of Lords are similar to those enjoyed by the House of Commons.

8.3 Recent cases and statutes

The important principle-making cases are referred to in the key points section. While there are occasions today when particular MPs are reported to the Committee of Privileges, they are reported for breaches established by these cases. While students should note headline making cases, they should only serve as further examples of existing principles.

8.4 Analysis of questions

This is an important subject and a question on this area in every examination paper can be expected. The question can either be a general essay question requiring a critical discussion of the topic or a problem solving exercise; if the latter, the popular question requires you to consider whether what a particular MP has said about someone comes within the meaning of a 'proceeding in Parliament' so as to be protected by parliamentary privilege and/or whether what a particular newspaper writes about an MP comes within the meaning of qualified privilege so as, once again, to be protected from attack.

8.5 Questions

QUESTION 1

'The two Houses justify the special rights, powers and immunities conferred by parliamentary privilege as being necessary for the welfare of the nation. Citizens denied legal redress against MPs or adjudged by the House of Commons to have committed a high contempt and a breach of its privileges tend to be less impressed by these claims'. (de Smith).

University of London LLB Examination
(for External Students) Constitutional Law June 1985 Q4

Skeleton solution

• Introduction: definition of parliamentary privilege; the justification for the privilege; examples of privileges.

• Cases of abuse where the Member hides behind privilege; example of freedom of speech in debate and the law of defamation.

• Procedure for determining breaches of privilege; punishments available to those found guilty of contempt or breach of privilege; procedure for dealing with complaints - breaches of the rules of natural justice; recommendations of the 1967 Select Committee on Parliamentary Privilege.

• General conclusion: breach of the rule of law; breach of natural justice.

Suggested solution

Parliamentary privilege forms part of the law and custom of Parliament evolved by the two Houses in order to protect their freedom to conduct their proceedings without improper interference by the Sovereign, the courts, or other bodies or persons outside Parliament. It is defined by Erskine May as 'the sum of the peculiar rights enjoyed by each House collectively as a constitutional part of the High Court of Parliament and by members of each House individually, without which they could not discharge their functions, and which exceed those possessed by other bodies or individuals'.

The privileges enjoyed by the House of Commons include those 'ancient and undoubted privileges' claimed by the Speaker at the beginning of each new Parliament such as freedom of speech in debate, freedom from civil arrest, freedom of access via the Speaker to the Sovereign and that the most favourable construction should be placed upon all their proceedings. There are also more privileges enjoyed by the House in its corporate capacity such as the right to regulate its own composition, the right to take exclusive cognisance of matters arising within the precincts of the House and the right to punish both Members and non-Members for breach of privilege and contempt. Similar provisions apply in respect of the House of Lords. These special rights, powers and immunities conferred by parliamentary privilege are justified as being essential for the conduct of the business and the maintenance of the authority of the House.

There is no doubt, however, that while parliamentary privilege may be considered necessary for the welfare of the nation, there is wide scope for abuse by MPs especially as regards freedom of speech. Article 9 of the Bill of Rights 1689 provides that the freedom of speech, and debates or proceedings in Parliament ought not to be imposed or questioned in any court or place out of Parliament. Therefore no action or prosecution can be brought against a member for any words used in the course of parliamentary proceedings. If a Member were to be sued for libel or slander in respect of words used in Parliament in the course of 'proceedings in Parliament', the writ should be struck out as disclosing no cause of action. If the case were to come to trial the court would hold that the Member was protected by absolute privilege in the law of defamation. Thus, an MP may make defamatory statements regarding an individual, in the course of proceedings in Parliament, knowing that even if there is no basis to his allegations he is protected from a civil action for damages in tort. No action would be against him even if his remarks were shown to be defamatory, untrue, malicious and unfair, no matter how much damage is caused to the individual as a result.

Further, the House still reserves to itself the right to treat the institution of legal proceedings against a Member in respect of a matter covered, in its opinion, by parliamentary privilege, as a breach of its own privilege and may punish the individual concerned for breach of privilege or contempt. Of course, a Member who abuses his privilege of freedom of speech may be subject to disciplinary sanctions by the House, but this is not great deterrent. The fact remains that every year innocent individuals are defamed by ill-informed, careless or even malicious MPs and suffer considerable damage to their reputation as a result, but are nevertheless denied any legal redress because the MP concerned hides behind his parliamentary privilege.

Those individuals adjudged by the House to have committed a high contempt and a breach of its privileges are also treated in a manner which is open to considerable criticism. Parliamentary privileges are part of the common law in so far as their existence and validity are recognised by the courts. But they are enforced not by the courts but exclusively by Parliament.

By virtue of its inherent right to control its own proceedings and maintain its dignity, the House of Commons in protecting its privileges may punish those who violate them or commit contempt of the House. Breach of privilege consists of either an abuse of a particular privilege by a member, or any conduct which interferes with one of the privileges of Parliament. Contempt is a much wider concept and consists of any conduct which tends to bring the House into disrepute or detract from its dignity. No matter whether the offence is styled a breach of privilege or a contempt, or both, the penal powers of the House are the same. Offenders may be reprimanded or admonished by the Speaker. Members may be suspended or expelled. Officials of the House may be dismissed and any Member or stranger may be committed to prison for the duration of the parliamentary session. However, it is the procedure by which complaints of breach of privilege are dealt with which is open to most criticism.

Complaints of breach of privilege may be raised by a Member or in the House by the Speaker. If the Speaker rules that a prima facie case has been made out a motion is proposed that the matter be referred to the Committee of Privileges. The motion may then be debated and voted upon. The Committee, comprising the 15 most senior members of the parties in the House, is the master of its own proceedings. It can compel the attendance of witnesses and the production of documents, failure to comply being a contempt. There is no requirement of legal representation, indeed the 'defendant' may not be given any hearing at all. At the conclusion of its investigation the Committee reports its findings to the House and may recommend the action that the House should take. The House need not accept the Committee's findings nor recommendations, but it almost always does. This procedure has been criticised. The Select Committee on Parliamentary Privilege in 1967 recommended that persons directly concerned in the Committee's investigations should have the right to attend its hearings, make submissions, call, examine and cross-examine witnesses and, with leave of the Committee, be legally represented and apply for legal aid. These recommendations have however never been adopted.

It can be seen therefore that whatever the justification for parliamentary privilege may be, it is open to abuse by the less responsible members of the House, it is a breach of the rule of law, and the procedures for dealing with allegations of breach of privilege and contempt invariably breach the rules of natural justice. It is therefore an area ripe for reform.

QUESTION 2

The House of Commons has too wide a jurisdiction to punish contempts and breaches of privilege.

Discuss.

University of London LLB Examination
(for External Students) Constitutional law June 1984 Q5

General comment

This is a straightforward essay question requiring the student to show the relationship of Parliament to the courts as regards parliamentary privilege.

Skeleton solution

Parliamentary privilege:

- Courts decide what privileges exist;

- Parliament deals with breaches of such privileges.

Suggested solution

Parliamentary privilege is part of the law and custom of Parliament evolved by the two Houses in order to protect their freedom to conduct their proceedings without improper interference by the Sovereign, the courts, or the public. The privileges enjoyed by the House of Commons include those 'ancient and undoubted privileges' claimed by the Speaker at the beginning of each new Parliament such as freedom of speech in debate, freedom from civil arrest and freedom of access via the Speaker to the Sovereign. There are also those privileges enjoyed by the House in its corporate capacity such as the right to regulate its own composition and the right to regulate its own proceedings. These special rights, powers and immunities conferred by parliamentary privilege are justified as being essential for the conduct of the business and the maintenance of the authority of the House.

Parliamentary privileges are part of the common law in so far as their existence and validity are recognised by the courts. But they are enforced not by the courts but exclusively by Parliament. By virtue of its inherent right to control its own proceedings and maintain its dignity, the House of Commons in protecting its privileges may punish those who violate them or commit contempt of the House. Breach of privilege consists of either an abuse of a particular privilege by a Member or any conduct which interferes with one of the privileges of Parliament. Contempt is a much wider concept and consists of any conduct which tends to bring the House into disrepute or detract from its dignity. No matter whether the offence is styled a breach of privilege or a contempt, or both, the penal powers of the House are the same. Offenders may be reprimanded or admonished by the Speaker. Members may be suspended or expelled. Officials of the House may be dismissed and any Member or stranger may be committed to prison for the duration of the Parliamentary session. However, in discussing the jurisdiction of the House to punish for breach of privilege and contempt a distinction must be drawn between the two.

In the past questions of privilege have been a source of considerable conflict between the Commons and the courts. Indeed, the House still asserts that it is the absolute and sole judge of the extent of its own privileges and has invoked its historical status as part of the High Court of Parliament in claiming that its judgments are not examinable by any other court. But this is a claim to which the courts do not fully accede. While the courts recognise the control which the House has over its own proceedings, in *Stockdale v Hansard* (1839) the court maintained the right to determine the nature and the limits of parliamentary privilege when adjudicating upon the rights of individuals outside the House. The court also affirmed that the Commons cannot create new privileges by resolutions of the House, only by statute. Therefore, while the jurisdiction of the House of Commons to punish for breaches of privilege is wide, in the sense that the privileges are enforced exclusively by the House, nevertheless there are limitations, notably the court's power to determine whether the privilege arises and if so its scope and effect. In such cases privilege forms a part of the common law and is subject to it.

But while the House cannot by resolution enlarge the scope of its own privileges, it has not closed the categories of contempt. Therefore, while the courts may assert their jurisdiction to decide the existence and extent of privileges of the House, what constitutes a contempt of the House is essentially a matter which only the House can decide. If a contempt issue arises relating to the internal proceedings of the House, the courts will decline to interfere, and whether in relation to matters inside or outside the House, the courts have always recognised the power of the House to imprison for contempt. It is accepted today that where the cause of committal stated in the return to the writ is insufficient in law, the court may review. But if no cause for committal other than the simple statement of contempt of the House is shown in the return, the court will not make further inquiry into the reasons for the committal. Therefore the jurisdiction of the House of Commons to punish for contempt is very wide. The House has power to commit persons for contempt for whatever conduct it adjudges to amount to contempt, provided that the cause of the contempt is not stated.

QUESTION 3

Jones is an MP for the constituency of Westhampton which for some time has suffered from a deterioration in relations between the police and the immigrant community. Recently Jones received a letter from a constituent complaining that he had been beaten up by one PC Plod for no reason whatsoever other than the fact that he was black. (This allegation was completely untrue). Jones decided this was an opportunity to get to grips with the race relations problem and wrote three letters: one to a minister in the Home Office; one to the Westhampton Weekly; and one to the Community Relations Officer of the Local Authority. All the letters repeated the allegation as if it was pure fact. Jones also repeated the allegation in a question to the Secretary of State for the Home Office made during parliamentary question time and the question was reported in the Daily Garble the next day. Jones has also recently been offered a post with the Equality for Immigrants Association in which he is to be paid £5,000 per annum and he is expected to always support measures furthering the interests of the Association.

PC Plod has recently issued writs against the constituent, the Daily Garble and Jones complaining he has been libelled. Furthermore, the Speaker of the House has become aware of the offer of employment made by the EIA.

Discuss the foregoing in the light of the law relating to parliamentary privilege.

Written by Editor 1990

Skeleton solution

Introduction

- Outline nature and basis of parliamentary privilege.

- State types of privilege raised by question ie freedom of speech, freedom from interference.

- State that the question raises following:

  is letter from constituent privileged?

  are letters from Jones privileged?

  is report by Daily Garble protected by qualified privilege?

  is employment with EIA against freedom from interference?

Letter from constituent

- Probably not absolutely privileged: *Rivlin* v *Bilainkin* (1953).

- May attract qualified privilege - *R* v *Rule* (1937) - but is he acting maliciously?

Letters from Jones

Which ones fall within meaning of 'proceeding in Parliament'?

- question in house - yes: *Church of Scientology* v *Smith* (1972); *Case of GWR Strauss MP* (1957).

- letter to Home Office - yes: *Attorney-General for Ceylon* v *De Livera* (1963).

- letter to Westhampton Weekly - no.

- letter to Community Relations Officer - no.

Daily Garble Report

Probably attracts qualified privilege: s7 Defamation Act 1954; *Cook* v *Alexander* (1974); *Beach* v *Freeson* (1972).

The offer of employment

Jones is restricted in how he can act and also is receiving a payment. Accordingly this offer probably does interfere with his freedom as an MP and would be a contempt: *Case of DFS Henderson MP* (1945); *Case of WJ Brown MP* (1947).

Suggested solution

In order for MPs to function properly they must be able to carry out their duties freely and without fear of being sued for defamation. Such protections come within the ambit of parliamentary privilege. This question raises two particular privileges as far as Jones is concerned: freedom of speech and freedom from interference. It is also in the public interest that constituents in their complaints to Members of Parliament and newspapers reporting parliamentary matters should also receive a degree of protection from the possibility of being sued for libel. This question also demands a discussion of the extent to which such persons are protected by qualified privilege.

Turning firstly to the letter to Jones from the constituent, in *R* v *Rule* (1934) the appellant wrote a letter to the MP containing defamatory statements about a police officer and a magistrate. It was held that such a letter may attract qualified privilege ie so long as the author was not notified by malice he could not be sued for defamation. Further in *Rivlin* v *Bilainkin* (1953) it was suggested that if such a letter concerned matters currently being discussed by Parliament it might be absolutely privileged. On the facts of the instant case since the allegation by the constituent is completely untrue it is difficult to see how he can be said not to be acting maliciously and, therefore, he is likely to be held liable to PC Plod.

As regards the actions by Jones, whether he is absolutely privileged depends on whether they fall within the meaning of 'proceedings in Parliament'. Clearly the question raised in the House of Commons must be a 'proceeding in Parliament' and would be privileged: *Church of Scientology* v *Smith* (1972). In the *Attorney-General for Ceylon* v *De Livera* (1963) Viscount Radcliffe stated that it was not only proceedings on the floor of the House that were covered by the expression 'proceedings in Parliament'. His Lordship considered that an MP was protected whenever he was carrying out his 'real' or 'essential' functions as an MP.

It would seem that the letter to the Minister for the Home Office would come within the 'real' or 'essential' functions of Jones and, therefore, be privileged. Support for this can be found in the *case of GWR Strauss MP* (1957). In this case Strauss wrote to the Paymaster General about a nationalised industry. The Select Committee held this letter to be privileged although the matter was then referred to the full House of Commons which decided it was not privileged. However, it is now felt that it would be deemed to be privileged.

On the basis of the above, however, it is doubtful whether the letters to the Westhampton Weekly and the Community Relations Officer can be deemed 'proceedings in Parliament' and would not, therefore, be privileged.

The Daily Garble has reported a 'parliamentary proceeding' namely the question in the House. The Defamation Act 1954 preserves the right of newspapers to accurately and fairly report such proceedings. Such reporting attracts qualified privilege and, since there is no suggestion of malice by the Daily Garble, it will be protected from the defamation action by PC Plod: *Cook* v *Alexander* (1974).

Finally the offer of employment by the Equality for Immigrants Association has to be considered. Jones is to be paid £5,000 for always supporting measures that further the interests of the Association. Two cases fall to be considered in deciding whether this arrangement would be in breach of the privilege against interference.

In the *Case of DFS Henderson* (1945) Henderson asked an MP for help in his negotiations with the Ministry of Agriculture. He offered to pay 100 guineas to the MP's local association if the negotiations were successful. Was this a bribe and, therefore, a contempt of Parliament? It was held that since the payment was not to the MP personally and also because the MP's permission to make such a payment was sought beforehand that there was no contempt. However, such a practice was deemed to be generally objectionable. And in the *Case of WJ Brown* (1947) the MP had been elected General Secretary of the Civil Service Union on condition that it did *not* affect his political independence and that he did *not* have to represent the views of the union. Brown fell out with the Union who voted to remove him as its General Secretary. Brown complained that the Union was trying to interfere with his independence as an MP and was, therefore, in contempt. It was held that Brown had voluntarily placed himself in his position and the actions of the Union could not amount to a contempt.

In Jones' case he clearly is receiving a direct payment and, further, is limiting his political independence because he would have to vote in support of measures in the interests of the EIA whether he agreed with them or not. It is likely, therefore, that the Speaker would report him to the Committee of Privileges if he accepted the employment and that he would be held to be in contempt. Whilst the Committee has powers to expel and fine Members of Parliament it is often the case that MPs are let off with little more than a stern warning.

9 THE EXECUTIVE

9.1 Introduction

9.2 Key points

9.3 Recent cases and statutes

9.4 Analysis of questions

9.5 Questions

9.1 Introduction

The Executive includes the monarchy, ministers, central government, the Civil Service, armed forces and the police. The monarchy is bound by convention and executive functions are largely exercised by ministers (see chapter 10: *The Royal Prerogative*). With the advent of the Cabinet, policies decided by government form the basis of legislation passed by Parliament. The Prime Minister enjoys enormous powers because of her position as head of the Cabinet.

9.2 Key points

a) *The Prime Minister*

  i) Formal position of the Prime Minister

  • The office of Prime Minister is a de facto institution recognised by statute but governed mainly by convention.

  • The office of Prime Minister is invariably held together with the office of First Lord of the Treasury: Ministerial and Other Salaries Act 1975.

  • On the creation of the Civil Service Department in 1968 the Prime Minister became Minister for the Civil Service.

  ii) Choosing a Prime Minister

  • The choice of Prime Minister is a matter for the Queen alone in the exercise of the Sovereign's personal prerogative.

  • By convention however the Queen should choose that person who is able to command the support of the majority in the House of Commons.

  iii) Functions of the Prime Minister

  • Formation of the government: Ministers are appointed by the Queen on the advice of the Prime Minister. All ministers must be or become members of one or other House of Parliament. There may be up to 95 holders of ministerial office in the House of Commons: House of Commons Disqualification Act 1975.

- **Formation of the Cabinet:** The choice of Cabinet is a matter entirely in the Prime Minister's discretion, although her choice will be influenced by political expediency.

- **Presiding over Cabinet meetings:** The Prime Minister presides over full Cabinet meetings and also over meetings of the most important committees of the Cabinet. The Prime Minister decides the agenda for Cabinet meetings and controls discussion within the Cabinet. At the conclusion of a Cabinet meeting no formal vote is taken on the policy decided; it is for the Prime Minister to sum up the consensus opinion. The Cabinet Secretariat is directly responsible to the Prime Minister and the allocation of functions between Cabinet, committees of the Cabinet and individual departments is controlled by her.

- **The organisation and control of central government:** The Prime Minister decides how government functions should be allocated between departments and may create, amalgamate or abolish government departments. The Prime Minister may also take an interest in the affairs of particular departments and intervene personally in major issues and take decisions without consulting Cabinet.

- **Powers of patronage:** By convention the Prime Minister advises the Queen on the granting of peerages and other honours and on appointments to certain high offices of state.

- **Advising the Sovereign:** The Prime Minister is the main channel of communication between the Cabinet and the Sovereign, and it is her duty to keep the Queen informed on matters of State.

- **Presentation and defence of government policy:** Prime Minister's interventions in debate always attract media attention. The Prime Minister also controls government communications and the dissemination of information.

b) *The Cabinet*

i) Composition of the Cabinet

The number of ministers in the Cabinet is the sole choice of the Prime Minister. Usually it comprises between 18 and 23 members. The composition of the Cabinet is also a matter for the Prime Minister's discretion. However by convention and custom certain ministers are always members of the Cabinet.

ii) Conventions relating to Cabinet government

- The Queen must act on the advice of Her Ministers.

- The Cabinet must always tender unanimous advice.

- The Cabinet must obtain and maintain a majority in the House of Commons on all major matters of policy.

81

- The Cabinet must produce a 'Queen's Speech' at the opening of each session of Parliament, stating the legislation which it proposes during that session.

- The 'mandate' doctrine requires the government's statement in the Queen's speech to be consistent with the policy on which they were elected.

iii) Cabinet committees

A complicated system of Cabinet committees exists to facilitate the discussion and formulation of policy options and to co-ordinate the activities of the various government departments, with regard to policy.

iv) The Cabinet Secretariat

In 1917 a Secretary to the Cabinet was appointed to service Cabinet and Cabinet committee meetings, take minutes and circulate details of conclusions reached in Cabinet. The Secretariat is headed by the Permanent Secretary to the Cabinet Office who is directly responsible to the Prime Minister.

v) Prime Minister's Policy Unit

The Prime Minister maintains a Policy Unit in Downing Street, independent of the Cabinet Office.

vi) Cabinet Secrecy

As all ministers must support government policy it is desirable that the process by which such policy decisions are made be kept secret, unless the Prime Minister decides otherwise, therefore secrecy is attached to discussions in Cabinet, Cabinet papers and the proceedings of Cabinet committees.

c) *Prime ministerial or Cabinet government?*

i) The Cabinet is the engine house of government. Administrative action is co-ordinated and legislative initiatives sanctioned in the Cabinet. Cabinet can therefore exert significant control over Parliament.

However the special position enjoyed by the Prime Minister has led some authorities to the conclusion that Cabinet government has now given way to Prime Ministerial government.

ii) The power of Prime Minister relative to the Cabinet depends upon several factors:

- The personality of the particular Prime Minister.

- The standing of the Prime Minister both in Parliament and in the Party.

- Whether the Prime Minister is minded to take full advantage of the conventional powers available to the holder of the office.

d) *Collective responsibility*

The doctrine of collective responsibility involves two rules:

i) The rule that the government must resign if it loses the support of the House of Commons.

The Prime Minister and her ministers are collectively responsible to Parliament for the conduct of national affairs. If the Prime Minister loses support in Parliament she must resign or seek a dissolution of Parliament.

ii) The rule that the government must speak with one voice.

- All members of the government share in the collective responsibility of the government, and ministers may not publicly criticise or dissociate themselves from the government policy.

- A Cabinet Minister who feels unable to agree with his colleagues should resign.

- The rule is closely related to that of Cabinet secrecy. As all ministers must support government policy it is desirable that the process by which such policy decisions are made be kept secret.

- The rule increases party discipline and unity within the government and also serves to strengthen the authority of the Prime Minister in relation to her colleagues.

e) *Agreements to differ*

Occasionally it may be politically impossible for the Cabinet to maintain a collective front.

i) The National Government 1932: The Liberal members of the National Government only agreed to remain in the government on condition that they were allowed to speak and vote against it on the question of the imposition of tariffs.

ii) The Labour Government 1975: The Labour Cabinet 'agreed to differ' on the question of the United Kingdom's continued membership of the EEC.

f) *Individual responsibility*

Ministers are responsible to Parliament for their own actions, omissions and mistakes as well as for those of the officials in their departments. Normally criticism should be directed at the minister rather than at any civil servant who may be at fault. This principle is said to help preserve the anonymity, and therefore the objectivity and efficiency, of the Civil Service.

i) Ministerial responsibility for departmental maladministration

Two questions arise from the minister's departmental responsibility:

- Is the minister obliged to accept responsibility for every piece of maladministration within his department?

- If maladministration if found to have occurred is the minister under a duty to resign?

ii) Situations in which a minister must accept responsibility

In a debate on the Crichel Down Affair 1954, the Home Secretary stated his views as to when a minister must accept responsibility and not blame his civil servants:

- A minister must protect a civil servant who has carried out his explicit orders.

- A minister must defend a civil servant who acts properly in accordance with the policy laid down by the minister.

- Where an official makes a mistake or causes some delay, but not on an important issue of policy and not where a claim to individual rights is seriously involved, the minister acknowledges the mistake and he accepts the responsibility although he is not personally involved.

- Where action has been taken by a civil servant of which the minister disapproves and has no previous knowledge, and the conduct of the official is reprehensible, there is no obligation on a minister to endorse what he believes to be wrong or to defend what are clearly shown to be errors of his officers. He remains, however, constitutionally responsible to Parliament for the fact that something has gone wrong, but this does not affect his power to control and discipline his staff.

iii) Is there a duty to resign?

There is no suggestion that a minister has to resign if he does accept responsibility. Whether a minister has to resign or not depends upon a variety of political factors including:

- the temperament of the minister;
- the attitude of the Prime Minister; and
- the mood of the party and the tone of the Opposition.

g) *The courts and ministerial responsibility*

While the courts cannot enforce the convention of ministerial responsibility they are prepared to acknowledge its existence: *Carltona Ltd v Commissioners of Works* [1943] 2 All ER 560.

9.3 Recent cases and statutes

An up-to-date knowledge of political affairs as they affect the role of the Prime Minister and government ministers is important.

The Westland Affair - resignation of Defence Secretary.

The Falklands Campaign - resignation of Foreign Secretary.

9.4 Analysis of questions

Questions are essay type and often test students' knowledge of the conventions of ministerial responsibility. A good understanding of the function of Parliament and accountability of government is required.

9.5 Questions

QUESTION 1

To what extent, if at all, is it true to say that the conventions of individual and collective ministerial responsibility are twins and yet incompatible?

University of London LLB Examination
(for External Students) Constitutional Law June 1986 Q6

General comment

This question involves discussion of the conventions of collective and individual responsibility and comment upon the inter-relationship between them, in particular the overlaps which seem to exist in their application.

Skeleton solution

- Introduction - the doctrine of responsible government.

- Collective responsibility; the content and application of, and the justification for, the convention.

- Individual responsibility; the content and application of, and the justification for, the convention.

- The possibility for conflict in the application of collective and individual responsibility.

Suggested solution

Democracy requires that those who govern should be responsible to those whom they govern. The convention of ministerial responsibility seeks to achieve this aim. It has two aspects. Firstly, the collective responsibility of the government as a whole to Parliament and, secondly the individual responsibility of ministers to Parliament for decisions, taken in their departments, whether by themselves or by their civil servants.

The doctrine of collective responsibility involves two rules. Firstly, it is accepted that the government must resign if it loses the support of the House of Commons. The Prime Minister and her ministers are collectively responsible to Parliament for the conduct of national affairs. If the Prime Minister loses support in Parliament she must resign or seek a dissolution of parliament. The rule does not mean that the government must resign whenever it is defeated on any issue. There has to be a clear-cut defeat for the government on a matter of policy.

Secondly, the doctrine of collective responsibility involves the rule that the government must speak with one voice. All members of the government share in the collective responsibility of the government, and ministers may not publicly criticise or dissociate themselves from government policy. The essence of collective responsibility is that the Cabinet should be seen to be in agreement: a Cabinet Minister who feels unable to agree with his colleagues should resign. The constitutional justification for the rule is that the answerability of the government to Parliament would be severely impaired if individual ministers were able to say that they personally did not agree with decisions taken in Cabinet. Ministers, including non-Cabinet members, are normally bound therefore not to differ publicly from Cabinet decisions nor to speak or vote against the government in Parliament. The rule increases party discipline and unity within the government, strengthens the government in Parliament and reinforces the secrecy of decision making within the Cabinet thereby minimising public disagreement between both ministers and departments of state. It also serves to strengthen the authority of the Prime Minister in relation to her colleagues.

The convention of individual responsibility requires that ministers are responsible to Parliament for their own actions, omissions and mistakes as well as for those of the officials in their departments. This principle is said to help preserve the anonymity and therefore the objectivity and efficiency of the civil service. Thus, Government Bills are introduced into Parliament by the departmental ministers, who are responsible for the proposals they contain. In debates concerning the work of individual departments, the minister concerned is expected to reply to the criticisms raised and usually seek to defend the department. Ministers are also expected to meet the reasonable requests of members for information concerning their departments and answer questions relating to their departments at question time.

It can be seen therefore that in many respects the relationship between individual and collective responsibility is very close and to this extent they may be viewed as twins. However, there is also in some respects a high degree of incompatibility between the two. For instance, if responsibility for making of policy decisions lies collectively with the whole government, is it not inconsistent to hold the departmental minister individually responsible for the implementation of that policy? Many of the decisions announced by a minister will have been taken or approved in Cabinet or by Cabinet committees and to this extent the doctrine of collective responsibility will attach to them. Similarly, while a departmental minister may have the authority to make decisions relating exclusively to the sphere for which he is responsible, on many matters he may have to consult with other departments, for example the Treasury. Should that minister then be held responsible for the consequences? Conversely, if a minister is facing censure in Parliament as a result of his departmental policies, he may be individually responsible and accountable to Parliament, but he can nevertheless expect to receive the support of his governmental colleagues by bringing collective responsibility into play.

Of course, both individual and collective responsibility are rules of convention governed largely by political expediency and in consequence their practice may bear little relation to their theory. While their theory therefore may give an impression of incompatibility, the practical application of these conventions, looked at in their political context and judged on their particular facts, may explain the apparent incompatibility.

QUESTION 2

Explain the following:

'Much has been written about the collective and individual responsibilities of ministers. And sometimes the responsibilities of Cabinet Ministers are especially talked of. Several different ideas are involved in these matters and must be distinguished.'

University of London LLB Examination
(for External Students) Constitutional Law June 1985 Q6

General comment

This is a relatively straightforward question but it will require some detailed knowledge of instances of collective or individual responsibility to illustrate the answer. A definition of 'responsibility' in this context is required at the outset, followed by discussions of individual and collective responsibility. Notice that the question asks you to distinguish not only individual/collective responsibility of ministers but also responsibilities of Cabinet Ministers as opposed to ordinary ministers. Remembering that these are conventional rules one could conclude that the application of them depends on the strength of the Prime Minister and government involved.

Skeleton solution

- Introduction - the nature of the conventions of collective and individual responsibility.

- Practical application of the conventions with examples:

  individual responsibility - note political forces at work and the attitude of the PM;

  collective responsibility - note the notion of cabinet secrecy.

Suggested solution

Many of the British electorate at some time or another probably feel that a minister has behaved 'irresponsibly' or that the whole government has behaved 'irresponsibly' but this criticism would have little to do with a disregard for the concepts of individual and collective responsibility. Used in the context in question 'responsibility' seems to mean 'accountable' or 'answerable' but such definitions are still blurred and vague. Individual and collective responsibility are undoubted constitutional conventions and can be outlined in effect and illustrated by example but political practice often intervenes to leave doubts as to their application.

The principle of individual responsibility developed before the doctrine of collective responsibility. It states that all ministers, whether in or outside the Cabinet are responsible for their personal acts, the conduct of their departments and acts done or omissions by their departments.

The minister used to be legally responsible for damages that resulted to individuals as a result of the department's activity. Since the Crown Proceedings Act 1947 it has been possible to sue the Crown as the minister's employer and so today this aspect of individual responsibility is of little practical importance.

Ministers are answerable in the Commons in respect of matters lying within their field of responsibility which is either determined by statute or by convention. They are responsible not only for their personal acts but for the conduct of the departments. The area of 'responsibility' is easy to determine if laid down by legislation establishing the position and granting powers and duties to it. If a minister has no power or duty to take any action with regard to a matter, he cannot properly be held accountable to Parliament for what is done. Some ministers are assigned powers and duties by convention eg the Secretary of State for Foreign and Commonwealth Affairs which is a 'non-statutory' post, the Home Secretary has the prerogative of pardon and the Attorney-General the decision to enter a nolle prosequi. These conventions are well established and survive changes of government.

'Responsible to Parliament' cannot be easily defined. Public or private conduct unbecoming to a Minister of the Crown raises an expectation of a resignation. There are many examples of an acknowledgement of individual ministerial responsibility in this type of case. Earl Jellicoe and Lord Lampton resigned in 1973 following revelations that they had 'leaked' the Budget proposals. If there has been bad judgment or maladministration in the department some ministers feel it is their duty to resign. Whether this will be readily accepted depends on the personal authority of the Prime Minister at the time. With the Prime Minister's support a minister can 'brave the storm'. However when the storm has passed the minister may find himself reshuffled into a back seat office, or suddenly 'promoted' to the Lords or asked for his resignation at a less embarrassing moment for the government. In answering questions he is not expected to accept blame whenever a departmental official has committed a dishonest act or disobeyed instructions. He does 'carry the can' to some extent in having to answer the questions and publicly explain what has occurred. If maladministration is attributed to bad organisation and the minister ought to have been able to prevent it he will be in some degree blameworthy and may resign. There are recent examples of this. Sir Thomas Dugdale in 1954 resigned as Minister of Agriculture after allegations of maladministration by senior officials (the Crichel Down Affair). Lord Carrington resigned from the Foreign Ministry in 1982 having failed to predict and prepare for the Falklands invasion by the Argentinians. James (now Lord) Callaghan resigned in 1967 from the office of Chancellor of the Exchequer having finally failed to save the pound from devaluation but was immediately transferred to Home Secretary. In contrast however, Lord Whitelaw did not consider resignation from his position as Home Secretary over the Palace intruder. This area of individual responsibility depends not only on the Prime Minister and minister concerned, but also on how far the minister is identified by the public with the mistake or policy in question.

Finally being 'responsible to Parliament' has helped preserve the anonymity of civil servants but this is gradually being eroded. The select committees of the House of Commons and the Parliamentary Ombudsman, both recent innovations, single out identifiable civil servants. Nevertheless ministerial responsibility remains a protective cloak for the Civil Service.

The collective responsibility of government, Cabinet and Prime Minister starts with the principle that they should resign if they lose confidence of the House of Commons. This is not simply if the government is defeated on an issue, it must be a major issue of policy. Since 1924 only two governments, both in a minority in the Commons, have resigned in accordance with the convention. In 1924 Ramsay MacDonald's first Labour government found itself deserted by its Liberal allies and resigned. The then Mr Callaghan, who took over a tiny Labour majority in 1976, lost his majority through by-election defeats and defections and was finally defeated by a Conservative vote of no confidence in 1979. Such minority governments are extremely rare under our present system of electoral representation.

Collective responsibility also implies that all Cabinet Ministers assume responsibility for Cabinet decisions. In short the Cabinet must speak with one voice. This is where a Cabinet Minister's responsibility may become more onerous than that of a non-Cabinet minister. If a Cabinet Minister wishes to disagree in public he should first resign. The application of this convention again varies with the character of the Prime Minister - indiscretions can be overlooked. During the 1974-79 Labour Government some Cabinet Ministers received a timely reminder in the form of a minute issued by Harold Wilson to those concerned reminding them of the doctrine of collective Cabinet responsibility. This convention has been expressly waived three times in recent years. In 1975 over the referendum for the EEC and in 1978 over the European Assembly Elections Act there was an agreement to disagree. In 1978 Mr Callaghan is reported as saying 'I certainly think the doctrine should apply except in cases where I announce that it does not'. The earliest example was the 'National' government in 1932: to allow the coalition to vote at will was a disaster and failed after a few months.

This 'one voice' requires as a corollary Cabinet secrecy. From time to time the principles of Cabinet secrecy are disregarded by what seem to be deliberate leaks by ministers to the press. Leaking may be resorted to by ministers or the Prime Minister to explain a split in the Cabinet. This secrecy and support for Cabinet decisions should continue after a government has been defeated or the minister has lost office but this principle is weak. If the minister decides to resign he is usually allowed to publish a reasoned letter of resignation and make a resignation speech in the Commons. In recent years the publication of memoirs including past Cabinet discussions has become quite common. The Sunday Times after a legal battle (*Attorney-General* v *Times Newspapers* (1974)) were allowed to publish the Richard Crossman diaries as being in the national interest to do so. Barbara Castle and Harold Wilson to name but two have since rushed into print.

It is not entirely true to say that non-Cabinet ministers are not subject to the 'one voice' restriction. In Attlee's government after the Second World War a number of non-Cabinet ministers were sacked for just such an offence. This again depends on the Prime Minister involved and the political climate at the time.

There is a reasonably clear distinction between collective and individual responsibility and each involves a number of different ideas and possibly some as strong as principles. Those surrounding collective responsibility frequently concern Cabinet Ministers but they can and are sometimes applied to the whole government. All these ideas, being creatures of convention, are subject to the whims and political position of the personalities involved and in particular to those of the Prime Minister.

QUESTION 3

'There are no conventions about ministerial responsibility. Ministers simply do what they, or the Prime Minister, want to do.'

Discuss.

Prepared by Holborn College 1989

General comment

A difficult question to answer well. Students need not only to give an account of the conventions of individual and collective responsibility, but also to have a good understanding of developments in British politics in the last 15 years, and then be able to give examples to show that much depended on the Prime Minister's attitude.

Skeleton solution

The conventions of individual and collective responsibility to Parliament - a statement of the traditional position with example.

An analysis of the more recent tendency for ministers to resign dependent on the factors such as the mood of the country, the support of the PM and the attitude of the minister concerned, with example.

Suggested solution

Democracy requires that those who govern should be answerable to those whom they govern. The convention of ministerial responsibility seeks to achieve this aim. It has two aspects. Firstly, the collective responsibility of the government as a whole to Parliament and, secondly the individual responsibility of ministers to Parliament for decisions taken in their departments whether by themselves or by their civil servants.

The doctrine of collective responsibility involves two rules. Firstly, it is accepted that the government must resign if it loses the support of the House of Commons. The Prime Minister and her ministers are collectively responsible to Parliament for the conduct of national affairs. If the Prime Minister loses support in Parliament she must resign or seek a dissolution of Parliament. The rule does not mean that the government must resign whenever it is defeated on any issue. There has to be a clear cut defeat for the government on a matter of policy or a vote of no confidence.

Secondly, the doctrine of collective responsibility involves the rule that the government must speak with one voice. All members of the government share in the collective responsibility of the government, and ministers may not publicly criticise or dissociate themselves from government policy. The essence of collective responsibility is that the Cabinet should be seen to be in agreement. A Cabinet Minister who feels unable to agree with his colleagues should resign. The constitutional justification for this rule is that the answerability of the government to Parliament would be severely impaired if individual ministers were able to say that they personally did not agree with the decision taken in Cabinet. Ministers, including non-Cabinet members and Parliamentary Private Secretaries are normally bound therefore not to differ publicly from Cabinet decisions nor to speak or vote against the government in Parliament. The rule increases party discipline and unity within the government, strengthens the government in Parliament and reinforces the secrecy of decision making within the Cabinet thereby minimising public disagreement between both ministers and the departments of State. It also serves to strengthen the authority of the Prime Minister in relation to her Cabinet colleagues.

The convention of individual responsibility requires that ministers are responsible to Parliament for their own actions, omissions and mistakes as well as for those of their officials in the department. This principle is said to help preserve the anonymity and therefore the objectivity and efficiency of the civil service. Thus, Government Bills are introduced into Parliament by the departmental ministers, who are responsible for the proposals they contain. In debates concerning the work of individual departments the minister concerned is expected to reply to the criticisms raised and usually seeks to defend the department. Ministers are also expected to meet the reasonable requests of members for information concerning their departments and answer questions relating to their departments at question time.

Both individual and collective ministerial responsibility are rules of convention governed largely by political expediency. It may therefore be true to observe that as regards responsibility, ministers simply do what they, or the Prime Minister, want to do. So long as they do not get into political difficulty no other sanction is available to compel compliance. The whole purpose of conventions is to introduce flexibility into the Constitution and ministerial responsibility, particularly individual responsibility, is perhaps one of the best examples of conventional flexibility in contemporary constitutional practice.

If one were to start with the classic exposition of individual ministerial responsibility stated by Maxwell-Fyfe in the Crichel Down debate and then contrast it with modern practice it is quite obvious that a fundamental change has taken place regarding the situations in which the minister must accept responsibility and not publicly blame the civil servant. For example when the Queen discovered an intruder in her bedroom at Buckingham Palace the Home Secretary as the Minister responsible for Palace Security was most reluctant to accept any responsibility for the lapse in security. He preferred to distinguish between defects of policy for which he was responsible and defects in the day to day administration of that policy which fell to civil servants. Likewise, the Secretary of State for Northern Ireland made a similar distinction when the IRA prisoners broke out of the Maze Prison. In the former case responsibility was passed by the minister to the Metropolitan Police Commissioner, and in the latter to the prison governor. Both ministers escaped political difficulties so one must assume that this now represents the current conventional practice.

One can of course defend this change on the grounds that as the minister within the new super departments relies more upon the expertise of his civil servants, the increased profile of the civil servants in decision making should be reflected in the civil servant accepting more public responsibility when things go wrong. Convention is merely adapting itself and evolving to meet this change; individual responsibility being still regulated by a set of rules which in appropriate circumstances will have to be obeyed, as Lord Carrington found out after the invasion of the Falkland Islands. One should also be wary of confusing ministerial resignations with the convention of individual responsibility. Resignation has never fallen under the convention and thus has always depended to a large extent upon the attitude of the individual minister and the Prime Minister in particular, but the attitude of fellow ministers and of government backbenchers also plays a role. The position of Leon Brittan, Secretary of State for Trade and Industry, during the Westland Affair in 1986 is an instructive example. Leon Brittan faced criticisms and calls for his resignation on three occasions and was finally forced into resignation. The first criticism was of an alleged breach of collective responsibility when the Secretary of State allegedly indicated to a senior executive of British Aerospace that it would be in the public interest if that company withdrew from the European Consortium (the inference being that it was in the national interest for the rival US rescue by Sikorsky Helicopters to go through) a breach of collective responsibility as the government's declared policy was one of neutrality. A letter was sent by British Aerospace to the Prime Minister to complain and the Secretary of State under close questioning in the House of Commons denied all knowledge of such a letter.

This misjudgment gave rise to calls for his resignation, but the Cabinet closed ranks to protect the Minister. Finally the Secretary of State was forced into resignation when it was discovered that without authority from the Law Officers he had authorised the leaking to the press of a letter addressed by them to Michael Heseltine, former Secretary of State for Defence. The Prime Minister and Cabinet again tried to close ranks to protect Mr Brittan but the Conservative backbenchers 1922 Committee resolved that it could no longer support his tenure of office and he was thus forced to resign.

Similarly with collective responsibility. Breach usually results in resignation but in some situations a breach will involve no adverse consequence. There may even be waivers of collective responsibility. During the period of the Labour government in the 1970s waivers were granted in respect of the Referendum on EEC Membership in 1975 and the European Assembly Elections in 1978. In both cases these were necessitated by the precarious position of the government which was split over the issue. The essence of convention is flexibility and occasional breaches and waivers of collective responsibility do not remove the underlying convention. Its continued existence can be seen in the resignation of Michael Heseltine, Secretary of State for

Defence, during the Westland Affair in 1986 and in recent dismissals and resignations in the Labour Shadow Cabinet over differences in policy.

There is in many respects a degree of incompatibility between collective and individual responsibility. For example, if responsibility for the making of policy decisions lies collectively with the whole government, is it not inconsistent to hold the departmental minister responsible for the implementation of that policy? Many of the decisions announced by a minister will have been taken or approved in Cabinet or by Cabinet Committee and to this extent the doctrine of collective responsibility will attach to them. So why should the Prime Minister when things go wrong be able to divert attention from the government by passing responsibility to the departmental Minister. Undoubtedly this happens and once again it is accommodated within the flexible confines of convention. If the convention of collective responsibility is serving a purpose then some sanction will follow its breach. But again so long as no political difficulties ensure, so what.

Therefore it may be true to say that ministers simply do what they, or the Prime Minister, want to do. But there are conventional rules relating to ministerial responsibility which in appropriate circumstances will have to be obeyed if political difficulties are not to follow for those in breach.

10 THE ROYAL PREROGATIVE

10.1 Introduction

10.2 Key points

10.3 Recent cases

10.4 Analysis of questions

10.5 Questions

10.1 Introduction

The royal prerogative is important historically as being the original source of what we would now term governmental power. Before Parliament came into existence all government power came from and was administered by the monarch. Since 'the King could do no wrong' it was the rule that the courts could not question the exercise of such prerogative power.

Some personal prerogatives are still, in theory, retained by the monarch eg the power:

a) to award knighthoods and other honours (ie patronage);

b) to dissolve Parliament;

c) to appoint/dismiss Ministers;

d) to assent to Acts of Parliament.

In practice such personal prerogatives are theoretical rather than real in the sense that today the monarch would not exercise any of them without the advice of the Prime Minister.

All other prerogative powers have passed to and are exercised by the government of the day, and perhaps, should more properly called executive prerogatives. Of course most of the areas of power once governed by the prerogative have now been overtaken by Acts of Parliament which take precedence over the prerogative (*Attorney-General* v *De Keyser's Royal Hotel* [1920] AC 508). Since most government power has today been given by statute, the exercise of governmental powers are controllable by the courts by way of judicial review.

But what of those areas of government power that have not been overtaken by Act of Parliament and remain, therefore, within the prerogative? Can an individual complain to the courts about the way in which such powers have been exercised? This is the most topical aspect to the prerogative and the most likely examination area.

The major areas of such executive prerogative powers today are law and order, defence and foreign affairs. Sensitive matters of law and order, foreign policy and state security are probably still outside the scope of judicial review. For example in *Gouriet* v *The Union of Post Office Workers* [1977] 3 All ER 70 (concerning the refusal of the Attorney-General to take criminal action against power office workers refusing to sort mail going to South Africa); *China Navigation* v *Attorney-General* [1932] 2 KB 197 (concerning the manner in which the Government chose to protect its overseas nationals) and *Chandler* v *DPP* [1964] AC 763 (concerning the Government's nuclear defence policy) the courts felt unable to intervene.

However, the courts are naturally jealous of powers that cannot be challenged and in *BBC* v *Johns* [1965] Ch 32 the House of Lords stated that no new prerogative powers would be recognised by the courts. Indeed the 1970s onwards have seen a much more robust attitude by the courts towards the exercise of prerogative powers at least in matters of a more domestic and less sensitive nature. In *Laker Airways* v *Department of Trade* [1977] 2 All ER 182 which concerned the making of a treaty pertaining to air routes available to UK operators Lord Denning boldly stated:

'Seeing that the prerogative is a discretionary power to be exercised for the public good it follows that it's exercise can be examined by the courts just as any other discretionary power which is vested in the executive.'

Equating prerogative with statutory powers was going too far but the statement illustrates the court's dislike of unfettered powers. And such statements have led the courts in the 1980s to indicate that in certain areas they will question the merits of a decision made pursuant to the prerogative. It is now a matter of whether the area in question is one upon which the courts are competent to intervene. In a sensitive area the courts would not have the information or expertise to feel able to question a decision but, in other cases, the courts may well intervene as in the cases involving recognition of trade unions (*Council for Civil Service Unions* v *Minister for the Civil Service* [1984] 3 All ER 935, known as the GCHQ case), the use of weapons by the Police (*R* v *Secretary of State for the Home Department ex parte Northumbria Police Authority* [1988] 1 All ER 556) and the issue of passports (*R* v *Secretary of State for Foreign and Commonwealth Affairs ex parte Everett* [1989] 1 All ER 655).

10.2 Key points

It is important that students understand the following issues regarding the prerogative:

a) *Classification of the prerogative*

There are two traditional categories of prerogative:

   i) Personal prerogatives being those enjoyed by the Sovereign personally;

   ii) Political prerogatives being those exercised by or on the advice of the Crown.

b) *The effect of statute on the prerogative*

   i) Parliament is supreme. A prerogative can therefore be expressly abolished or restricted by statute.

   ii) The prerogative may not, however, be impliedly abolished by statute. The prerogative is merely placed in abeyance and if the statute is repealed the prerogative will be revived.

iii) If a statute conflicts with a prerogative without expressly abolishing the prerogative, the courts must give effect to the statute and treat the prerogative as being in abeyance: *Attorney-General* v *De Keyser's Royal Hotel* [1920] AC 508.

iv) A statute which conflicts with a prerogative may expressly provide that the prerogative be left intact.

c) *Prerogative and the courts*

Where the exercise of a prerogative directly affects the rights of an individual the courts may be asked to determine the following issues:

i) Does the prerogative claimed by the Crown exist? The courts will not recognise the existence of new prerogative powers. Only those already recognised at common law will be upheld: *BBC* v *Johns* [1965] Ch 32.

ii) Is the official or public body concerned entitled to benefit from the prerogative?

iii) Has the existence or exercise of the prerogative in question been affected by statute?

v) What is the extent of the prerogative power?

vi) Is it a prerogative which because of its nature and subject matter the court is competent to review? The traditional approach of the courts has been that while they may consider the existence, scope and extent of the prerogative they may not go further and review the merits of the exercise of the prerogative power. However recent cases indicate a shift in favour of granting judicial review in respect of the exercise of the prerogative in certain circumstances: *Council for Civil Service Unions* v *Minister for the Civil Service* [1984] 3 All ER 935; *R* v *Secretary of State for Home Department ex parte Northumbria Police Authority* [1988] 1 All ER 556; *R* v *Secretary of State for Foreign and Commonwealth Affairs ex parte Everett* [1989] 1 All ER 655.

10.3 Recent cases

R v *Secretary of State for the Home Department ex parte Northumbria Police Authority* [1988] 1 All ER 556

R v *Secretary of State for Foreign and Commonwealth Affairs ex parte Everett* [1989] 1 All ER 655

10.4 Analysis of questions

Questions are most likely to be essay type requiring the student to shown an understanding of the extent to which the courts are prepared to control the exercise of prerogative power.

10.5   Questions

QUESTION 1

To what extent, if any, did the House of Lords in the *Council of Civil Service Unions* v *Minister for the Civil Service* (GCHQ case) change the role of the judges in reviewing the royal prerogative?

University of London LLB Examination
(for External Students) Constitutional Law June 1987 Q6

Skeleton solution

* Introduction. Definition and examples of the prerogative.

* The traditional role of the courts in relation to the prerogative. The existence of the prerogative; its extent; who is entitled to its benefit; the effect of statute upon the prerogative; non-justiciability of a validly exercised prerogative.

* The implications of the GCHQ case. Situations in which the House of Lords may be prepared to review a prerogative act. The *Everett* (1989) case.

Suggested solution

According to Blackstone the prerogative is 'that special pre-eminence which the King has, over and above all other persons, and out of the ordinary course of the common law, in right of his royal dignity' (Blackstone, *Commentaries on the Laws of England*). Today the prerogative consists mainly of a miscellaneous collection of residual executive governmental powers which are considered to be necessary to enable the government to function. These are powers enjoyed by the Crown but not by the subjects of the Crown and include, for example, the power to conduct foreign relations, to declare war and make peace, to regulate the disposition of the armed forces, to appoint and dismiss ministers, to dissolve Parliament, to assent to Bills, to grant honours etc. The prerogative also includes certain immunities and privileges, such as the Queen's personal immunity from suit or prosecution.

Generally, the Executive derives its powers from two legal sources, statute and the prerogative. Where the Executive purports to act under powers conferred by statute, then, in the absence of any clause in the parent statute purporting to exclude the jurisdiction of the courts, the courts may review the action taken, and where necessary declare it void on the grounds of ultra vires or breach of natural justice. However, where the executive purports to act under the prerogative, and in so doing directly affects the rights of an individual, then traditionally the court's power is limited to the consideration of preliminary issues, namely the determination of the existence of the claimed prerogative and, if it is found to exist, its extent. This was for example the approach taken by the courts in such cases as *Attorney-General* v *De Keyser's Royal Hotel* (1920) and *Burmah Oil* v *Lord Advocate* (1965). Once it is established that the conduct complained of is an exercise of the prerogative, the courts cannot challenge its use. The only 'remedy' the aggrieved individual has is a political remedy, for example by trying to have the matter raised in Parliament.

The role of the judiciary in relation to the prerogative has therefore been limited to the consideration of preliminary issues. With regard to the existence of a purported prerogative act the court's main task is to ensure that no new prerogatives are created. Only those prerogatives already recognised at common law will be upheld. As Diplock LJ said in *BBC* v *Johns* (1965): 'It is 350 years and a civil war too late for the Queen's courts to broaden the prerogative. The limits within which the executive government may impose obligations or restraints on the citizens of the United Kingdom without any statutory authority are now well settled and incapable of extension'. If the prerogative claimed is found to exist then the court will next consider its extent.

Once it is established that the act complained of its an exercise of the prerogative the traditional view was the the courts cannot challenge its use. They can, however, seek to contain its exercise in accordance with common law principles. For example the courts can consider whether the body or person purporting to act under the prerogative is entitled to the benefit of the prerogative. To be entitled to the benefit of the prerogative the person or body concerned must be entitled by statute or otherwise to benefit from the privileges, rights or immunities of the Crown. The court must also consider whether the existence or exercise of the prerogative power has been affected by statute. For example the Crown Proceedings Act 1947 abolishes the immunity of the Crown from being sued in contract and tort, while leaving the personal immunity of the Sovereign intact. The prerogative may not, however, be impliedly abolished by statute. In such cases the prerogative is merely placed in abeyance and if the statute is repealed the prerogative will be revived. If a statute does conflict with a prerogative without expressly abolishing the prerogative, the courts must give effect to the statute and treat the prerogative as being in abeyance: see *Attorney-General* v *De Keyser's Royal Hotel* (1920). However, a statute which conflicts with a prerogative may expressly provide that the prerogative be left intact. For example, s33(5) of the Immigration Act 1971 provides that the powers conferred under the Act should be additional to any prerogative powers. Finally, the courts must consider whether the prerogative imposes a duty on the Crown to compensate the subject for damage caused by its exercise, as for example was the case in *Burmah Oil* v *Lord Advocate* (1965).

So while the courts were prepared to consider the existence and the extent of a purported prerogative power they traditionally declined to go any further and review the merits of the actual exercise of the prerogative. However, recent cases indicate a shift in favour of granting judicial review in respect of the exercise of the prerogative in certain circumstances. This view, first expressed by Lord Denning MR in *Laker Airways* v *Department of Trade* (1977), that the courts can intervene where a prerogative discretion is exercised improperly, was recently considered by the House of Lords in *Council for Civil Service Unions* v *Minister for the Civil Service* (1984), where their Lordships were called upon to consider whether the courts had the power to review, on the grounds of procedural irregularity, an instruction made in the exercise of a power conferred under the royal prerogative. Their Lordships were of the opinion that simply because a decision-making power was derived from a common law and not a statutory source it should not, for that reason only, be immune from judicial review.

According to Lord Diplock, judicial review had developed to a stage where one could classify under three heads the grounds on which administrative action was subject to control by judicial review: 'illegality, irrationality, and procedural impropriety.' As regards procedural impropriety, his Lordship saw no reason why it should not be a ground for judicial review of a decision made under powers of which the ultimate source was the prerogative.

However, Lord Roskill thought that the right of challenge could not be unqualified. It must depend upon the subject matter of the prerogative power that was exercised. Prerogative powers such as those relating to the making of treaties, the defence of the realm, the prerogative of mercy, the granting of honours, the dissolution of Parliament and the appointment of ministers, as well as others, were not, he thought, susceptible to judicial review because their nature and subject matter was such as not to be amenable to the judicial process. It was also pointed out that prerogative decisions would usually involve the application of government policy of which the courts were not the appropriate arbiters.

Their Lordships agreed therefore that executive action based on common law or the use of a prerogative power was not necessarily immune from review. This was especially so in the present case where the prerogative derived from an Order in Council, which was virtually indistinguishable from an order deriving from statute. In such cases the decision might be reviewed by the courts just as it would have been if it had rested on statutory powers. One such example was the issuing of passports under the prerogative, which was reviewed by the courts in the recent case of *R v Secretary of State for Foreign and Commonwealth Affairs ex parte Everett* (1989).

Therefore the GCHQ Case, in theory at least, does seem to have changed the role of the judges in reviewing the royal prerogative in that the fact that the source of executive power is the prerogative and not statute will not necessarily deprive the citizen of the right of challenge as to the manner of its exercise, providing that the nature and subject matter of the particular prerogative in question are considered by the courts to be susceptible to judicial review.

QUESTION 2

To what extent is it true to say today that the remedy for abuse of the prerogative lies in the political and not in the judicial field?

University of London LLB Examination
(for External Students) Constitutional Law June 1985 Q8

General comment

This question is based upon the relatively recent decision of the House of Lords in *Council for Civil Service Unions v Minister for the Civil Service* (GCHQ case) and concerns the powers of the courts to review the prerogative Acts of the Crown. Students should state the traditional role of the courts in relation to the royal prerogative and then consider the implications of the GCHQ case. This is a very straightforward and relatively easy prerogative question, but knowledge of the GCHQ case is vital. The approach of the House of Lords in the GCHQ case can be seen as another attempt by the judiciary to bring the Executive within the rule of law.

Skeleton solution

- Introduction: definition and examples of the prerogative.

- The traditional role of the courts in relation to the prerogative: the existence of the prerogative, its extent, who is entitled to its benefit, the effect of statute upon the prerogative; non-justiciability of a validly exercised prerogative.

- The implications of *Council for Civil Service Unions* v *Minister for the Civil Service*: situations in which the House of Lords may be prepared to review a prerogative act.

Suggested solution

According to Blackstone the prerogative is 'that special pre-eminence which the King has, over and above all other persons, and out of the ordinary course of the common law, in right of his royal dignity' (Blackstone, *Commentaries on the Laws of England*). Today the prerogative consists mainly of a miscellaneous collection of residual executive governmental powers which are considered to be necessary to enable the government to function. These are powers enjoyed by the Crown but not by the subjects of the Crown and include, for example, the power to conduct foreign relations, to declare war and make peace, to regulate the disposition of the armed forces, to appoint and dismiss ministers, to dissolve Parliament, to assent to Bills, to grant honours etc. The prerogative also includes certain immunities and privileges, such as the Queen's personal immunity from suit or prosecution.

The traditional view has been that where the Crown purports to act under the prerogative and in so doing directly affects the rights of an individual, the court's power is limited to determining the existence of the claimed prerogative and, if it is found to exist, its extent. Once it is established that the conduct complained of is an exercise of the prerogative, the courts cannot challenge it use. The only 'remedy' the aggrieved individual has is a political remedy, for example by trying to have the matter raised in Parliament.

The role of the judiciary in relation to the prerogative has therefore largely been limited to the consideration of preliminary issues. With regard to the existence of a purported prerogative act the court's main task is to ensure that no new prerogatives are created. Only those prerogatives already recognised at common law will be upheld. As Diplock LJ said in *BBC* v *Johns* (1965), 'It is 350 years and a civil war too late for the Queen's courts to broaden the prerogative. The limits within which the executive government may impose obligations or restraints on citizens of the United Kingdom without any statutory authority are now well settled and incapable of extension'. If the prerogative claimed is found to exist the court will next consider its extent. Problems may arise in the purported application of ancient prerogative powers in modern situations. For example, under the prerogative the Crown has the right to intercept postal communications. In *Malone* v *Metropolitan Police Commissioner*

(1979) the question arose as to whether this prerogative also justified the tapping of telephones. In such cases the courts must distinguish between the application of an established prerogative to new circumstances and the creation of an entirely new prerogative, which of course the courts will not allow.

Once it is established that the act complained of is an exercise of the prerogative the traditional view was that the courts cannot challenge its use. They can, however, seek to contain its exercise in accordance with common law principles. For example the courts can consider whether the body or person purporting to act under the prerogative is entitled to the benefit of the prerogative. To be entitled to the benefit of the prerogative the person or body concerned must be entitled by statute or otherwise to benefit from the privileges, rights or immunities of the Crown. The court must also consider whether existence or exercise of the prerogative power has been affected by statute. Parliament is supreme. A prerogative can therefore be expressly abolished or restricted by statute. For example the Crown Proceedings Act 1947 abolishes the immunity of the Crown from being sued in contract and tort, while leaving the personal immunity of the Sovereign intact. The prerogative may not, however, be impliedly abolished by statute. In such cases the prerogative is merely placed in abeyance and if the statute is repealed the prerogative will be revived. If a statute does conflict with a prerogative without expressly abolishing the prerogative, the courts must give effect to the statute and treat the prerogative as being in abeyance: see *Attorney-General* v *De Keyser's Royal Hotel* (1920). However, a statute which conflicts with a prerogative may expressly provide that the prerogative be left intact. For example, s33(5) of the Immigration Act 1971 provided that the powers conferred under the Act should be additional to any prerogative power. Finally, the courts must consider whether the prerogative imposes a duty on the Crown to compensate the subject for damage caused by its exercise, as for example was the case in *Burmah Oil* v *Lord Advocate* (1965).

But while the courts were prepared to consider the existence and the extent of a purported prerogative power they traditionally declined to go any further and review the merits of the actual exercise of the prerogative. However, recent cases indicate a shift in favour of granting judicial review in respect of the exercise of the prerogative in certain circumstances. This view, first expressed by Lord Denning MR in *Laker Airways Ltd* v *Department of Trade* (1977), that the courts can intervene where a prerogative discretion is exercised improperly, was recently considered by the House of Lords in *Council for Civil Service Unions* v *Minister for the Civil Service* (1984), where their Lordships were called upon to consider whether the courts had the power to review, on the grounds of procedural irregularity, an instruction made in the exercise of a power conferred under the royal prerogative. Their Lordships were of the opinion that simply because a decision making power was derived from a common law and not a statutory source it should not, for that reason only, be immune from judicial review.

However, Lord Roskill thought that the right of challenge could not be unqualified. It must depend on the subject matter of the prerogative power that was exercised. Prerogative powers such as those relating to the making of treaties, the defence of the realm, the prerogative of mercy, the grant of honours, the dissolution of Parliament and the appointment of Ministers, as well as others, were not, he thought, susceptible to judicial review because their nature and subject matter were such as not to be amenable to the judicial process. It was also pointed out that prerogative decisions would usually involve the application of government policy of which the courts were not the appropriate arbiters.

Their Lordships agreed, therefore, that Executive action based on common law or the use of a prerogative power was not necessarily immune from review. This was especially so in the present case where the prerogative derived from an Order in Council which was virtually indistinguishable from an order deriving from statute. In such cases the decision might be reviewed by the courts just as it would have been if it had rested on statutory powers.

Therefore while today it may still be true that the remedy for abuse of the prerogative will usually lie in the political and not in the judicial field, nevertheless there may be cases where the courts are prepared to question the exercise of the prerogative where its nature and subject matter are considered to be susceptible to judicial review. This trend may be seen as another attempt by the courts to bring the Executive within the rule of law.

QUESTION 3

'... it is necessary to consider what is meant by the expression "act of state", even if it is not expedient to attempt a definition'. (Lord Pearson, *Attorney-General* v *Nissan* [1970] AC 179, 237).

Discuss.

University of London LLB Examination
(for External Students) Constitutional Law June 1983 Q7

General comment

This is a difficult question requiring a discussion of the nebulous concept of 'act of state'. Students should describe what is generally meant by act of state although the whole subject suffers from a lack of clarity - be careful not to rely on old authorities which may have lost their meaning through passage of time. The only recent case (*Nissan*) should be discussed in some detail.

In conclusion students might like to question:

a)   Is there any modern justification for 'act of state'? Should the Crown not have to pay for what it takes in this day and age? Should it be preserved merely for acts against enemies?

b)   Is the idea of 'act of state' contrary to the rule of law? - is it reasonably precise? Are all men subject to the ordinary laws? Do the judges in *Nissan* fulfill their duties as guardians of the law?

Skeleton solution

- Define act of state.
- Explain importance of such action.
- Full discussion of *Attorney-General* v *Nissan*.

Suggested solution

Acts of state are primarily prerogative acts of policy in the field of external affairs - for example, the declarations of war, the conclusion of a treaty, an annexation of territory, the recognition of a foreign sovereign, state or government. But 'act of state' is used in many different senses and as yet no clear definition has been produced covering all aspects. Professor Wade's definition is similar to that above but observes that it is really only a construction put together from the decided cases - he feels the doctrine cannot be written down in terms of principle. Lord Wilberforce also says that the definition covers two rules: the first provides a defendant, normally a servant of the Crown, with a defence to an act otherwise tortious or criminal committed abroad provided that the act was authorised or subsequently ratified by the Crown; the second prevents courts taking cognisance of certain acts but this class of acts has not been accurately defined. It is unfortunate that the only modern case in which the Crown pleaded act of state as a defence in legal proceedings (*Attorney-General* v *Nissan* (1970)) was a disaster for students of law. The decision lacks any clear ratio and important questions were left half answered and points that seemed clear before the case have now been left uncertain. Following Lord Wilberforce's suggestion of a 'construction from decided cases' there follows a brief summary of what seems to be, or not to be meant by an act of state.

An act of state was, and probably still can be, pleaded by way of defence to an action in tort brought by an alien against the Crown for an act done outside British Dominion territory and authorised or subsequently ratified by the Crown - *Buron* v *Denman* (1848) an action of tresspass. Presumably this might be justified as the alien can seek redress from his own government. A friendly alien within the Dominions can successfully maintain an action against the Crown and act of state is consequently no defence: *Johnstone* v *Pedlar* (1921). An act of state is no defence to an act committed against a British subject within the Dominions (*Walker* v *Baird* (1892)) and it may be that an act of state is never a defence to an action by a British subject wherever he may be: see Lord Reid in *Attorney-General* v *Nissan* (1970).

These are the main 'principles' extracted from the major litigation in the last 150 years.

The cases suggest that the question whether an act was or was not an act of state is for the court to decide. This puts act of state in the same position as the rest of the royal prerogative - the courts cannot question the exercise of the prerogative nor the propriety of an act of state but it is for the court to decide whether or not an act falls within these categories. This would seem to make it 'expedient' to attempt a definition - without clear limits it leaves the Executive in a powerful position. Despite Lord Pearson's statement some attempt at 'clarification' was made by the

House of Lords in *Nissan* (1970) where the House decided by a majority on the point that the requisitioning and use of a hotel in Cyprus by British troops engaged in a peace-keeping operation was not within the category of 'act of state'. They did limit the concept of act of state from merely being an act of the UK Executive performed in the course of its relations with another state or with the subjects of another state. Lord Pearson suggested that it had to be 'something exceptional' and Lord Morris seemed to go along with that idea by suggested it was acting in 'a high-handed, extra-legal manner'. Lord Wilberforce's views are stated above and Lord Reid by defining it in terms of effect adds little.

It may be the defence of act of state can no longer be justified by the Executive. The idea of 'taking without giving' irrespective of the allegiance of the victim seems uncivilised, unmeritorious and indeed dangerous. With the exception of acts of war would the abandonment of 'act of state' leave a gap in the law? The limitations, such as they are, placed on the defence in *Nissan* perhaps indicate a judicial reluctance to accept what is an archaic abuse of power. However one must not read too much into the decision and remembering Lord Reid's 'executive-minded' judgment perhaps any judicial reluctance is being exaggerated.

Since so far as no judge has taken such a robust attitude as I would wish then it seems imperative that the parameters of this defence are carefully outlined. As it stands it seems to breach Dicey's first concept of the rule of law that all governmental powers shall be distributed and determined by reasonably precise laws. The extent to which an act is an act of state would seem wholly arbitrary. The defence might also be contrary to Dicey's second concept that no man is above the law. Once the defence has been established then the court will not question whether it is appropriate in the circumstances that there should be no compensation.

Whilst it is accepted that sensitive areas of foreign policy should not be subject to investigation by the courts it is important that such areas should be limited as much as possible. A blurred and confused definition of 'act of state' results in nothing but uncertainty as far as both litigants and judges are concerned.

Council under a duty to subsidise certain mini-bus services within its district but it has a discretion in that it need only make a subsidy where it is considered necessary to do so in the interests of the community. Where such a discretion is conferred on an authority the courts require, inter alia, that the discretion will be exercised for its proper purpose, ie that purpose envisaged by Parliament when it passed the parent Act, and that the discretion will be exercised reasonably.

In the present case whatever Ivan's real motive may be it is almost certain that the provision of transport to take old people shopping is one envisaged by Parliament as being in the interests of the community and it is also reasonable in the sense that it is a decision which a reasonable body would have taken.

QUESTION 2

Under s1 of the Wild Birds' Protection Act 1983 the Minister for Birds has 'power to make grants for the preservation of wild birds, if he in his opinion thinks that the furtherance of ecology demands it'. Under s2 'No grant shall be questioned in any court of law'.

The Minister, who is Chairman of the Puffins' Protection League, makes grants to the Budgerigars' Society and to the Puffins' Protection League. Hawk, who is an Opposition Member of Parliament and Secretary of the Woodpeckers' Club, applies for a grant, but is told by the Minister that he will not make a grant to any body associated with the Opposition. ·

Hawk wishes to challenge the grants to the Budgerigars' Society (on the grounds that a budgerigar is not a wild bird), and to the Puffins' Protection League, and to compel the Minister to consider the application of the Woodpeckers' Club.

Advise Hawk.

University of London LLB Examination
(for External Students) Constitutional Law June 1983 Q8

General comment

This is a relatively simple question on the basic grounds of challenge to administrative decisions. It is important to approach these type of questions logically. As with all the problems answer the question set and do not give long general discussions. You are to advise Hawk and not to write a general essay on administrative law.

Skeleton solution

*   a discussion of s2 and *Anisminic* v *Foreign Compensation Commission* (1969);

*   locus standi of Hawk especially following *IRC* v *National Federation of Self Employed and Small Businesses Ltd* (1982) case;

*   the specific challenges to the three decisions in question.

Suggested solution

The first problem Hawk faces in trying to challenge any of the Minister's decisions is that of s2 of the Act which seeks to exclude review by the High Court. However following the decision of *Anisminic* v *Foreign Compensation Commission* (1969) such an ouster clause will not operate where the challenge is to the jurisdiction of the tribunal or person making the decision. Jurisdiction has been conferred on the Minister to consider applications for grants in a fair and proper manner and acting on relevant and material considerations. If he has reached a wrong conclusion as to the width of his powers, or based on irrelevant matters, then that is an error of law as to his jurisdiction which is reviewable. An ultra vires decision to make a grant would be no grant at all and following the reasoning of *Anisminic* can be challenged in the High Court. The only 'exceptions' to this principle is where there is a statutory time limit (eg appeal etc must be within 28 days) as in *Smith* v *East Elloe RDC* (1956) or where the unreviewable decision is that of a judge - following *Re Racal Communications* (1981). The House of Lords judgment in *Re Racal Communications* is hard to understand but it suggests that where the ouster clause applies to the decision of a legally qualified judge then the clause will operate. Section 2 seems to be the basic ouster clause and as such it seems likely *Anisminic* would apply to allow review of the Minister's decisions.

To challenge any of the decisions Hawk must show that he has 'sufficient interest' in the matter under 0.53. The whole of locus standi for judicial review was recently discussed by the House of Lords in *IRC* v *National Federation of Self Employed and Small Businesses Ltd* (1982). In that case the Federation wished to challenge the amnesty granted by the IRC to 6,000 Fleet Street casual workers. They sought a mandamus to compel the IRC to assess these men for income tax. The question the House had to decide was had the Federation sufficient interest to bring such proceedings and the majority decided they had not. The reason is unclear. Lord Wilberforce suggests that the strength of the challenge should help determine locus so for reasons set out below as Hawk's challenge to the Budgerigars' Society is a strong one he may, by that fact alone, have sufficient locus. Wilberforce also suggests that a greater interest is required for mandamus than for certiorari. It may be that Hawk will have sufficient interest for the challenges to both the other societies.

The case suggests that unless locus is a simple issue it should not be taken as a preliminary point although this seems to be contrary to 0.53.

Hawk is Secretary of a competing Society and as the grants are available to a relatively small number in total (there are not that many bird protection societies), then it seems likely he would be considered to have sufficient locus. After all, if he cannot challenge a grant to the Budgerigars' Society then it is hard to think who could review the Minister's decision.

Lord Scarman and Lord Diplock both suggest a liberal approach to locus standi in the *IRC* v *National Federation of Self Employed and Small Businesses Ltd* case and it is to be hoped such an approach will be adopted in future.

Dealing firstly with the grant to the Budgerigar Society, this can be attacked as being simply ultra vires - a budgerigar is not a wild bird - and secondly as being an improper exercise of discretion. By simple statutory construction it seems unlikely that a budgerigar is a wild bird within the section and so a declaration would be granted. Following *Padfield* v *Minister of Agriculture Fisheries and Food* (1968) a discretion such as 'if he in his opinion thinks' in s1 must be exercised to further the purpose of the statute. I think the High Court would feel that no reasonable Minister could come to the conclusion that a grant to budgerigars would further 'ecology', and so it could be declared unlawful on that ground.

The grant to the Puffins' Protection League probably cannot be challenged. Puffins are wild birds. If Hawk can find evidence that the Minister was biased in making his decision then it could be challenged as being improper purposes but without such proof any challenge would fail. The courts will not presume that the Minister was biased merely from his position as chairman of the Puffins' Society. Unless proof can be found to show any of the separate grounds of challenge first outlined in *Associated Provincial Picture Houses* v *Wednesbury Corporation* (1948) then Hawk would be advised not to take proceedings on this matter.

Finally the refusal to hear the application of the Woodpeckers' Club can be challenged. Following *British Oxygen* v *Minister of Technology* (1971) the Minister has fettered his discretion and can be challenged for taking into account irrelevancies or again for using the statute for an improper purpose. Such a challenge would succeed.

As mandamus and certiorari do not lie against the Crown, Hawk should seek declarations to the effect that the grant to the Budgerigars was unlawful and that the refusal of his application was unlawful. In practice such declarations will be accepted by the Crown.

Type 2: An essay question requiring explanation of the classification of the grounds for judicial review expressed in *Council of Civil Service Unions* v *Minister for the Civil Service*.

QUESTION 3

When, and in what circumstances, will judges quash administrative decisions?

University of London LLB Examination
(for External Students) Constitutional Law June 1987 Q7

General comment

A rather general question concerning judicial review of administrative action.

Skeleton solution

- Introduction. Rules of the Supreme Court 0.53.

- Grounds for judicial review. Illegality; irrationality; procedural impropriety.

Suggested solution

An application for an order of certiorari to quash an administrative decision is made by way of an application to the High Court for judicial review under 0.53 of the Rules of the Supreme Court. The applicant must obtain leave of the court for his application to be heard and must establish the necessary locus standi, that is he must be shown to have a sufficient interest in the matter to which the application relates. If the court is satisfied as to the merits of the applicant's case and providing that the locus standi requirement is satisfied, it may then consider the substantive grounds on which judicial review may be exercised.

Generally speaking executive action will be the subject of judicial review on three separate grounds.

The first is where the authority concerned has been guilty of an error of law in its action, as for example purporting to exercise a power which in law it does not possess. The second is where it exercises a power in so unreasonable a manner that the exercise becomes open to review under the principles set out by Lord Greene MR in the case of *Associated Provincial Picture Houses Ltd* v *Wednesbury Corporation* (1948). The third is where it has acted contrary to what are often called the principles of natural justice. In the case of *Council of Civil Service Unions* v *Minister for the Civil Service* (1984) Lord Diplock devised a new nomenclature for each of these three grounds, calling them respectively 'illegality', 'irrationality' and 'procedural impropriety'.

In short, a decision will be 'illegal' if the decision maker has taken into account irrelevant matters in coming to his decision. According to Lord Diplock, whether he has or not is a justifiable question to be decided, in the event of dispute, by those persons, the judges, by whom the judicial power of the State is exercisable. It is a fundamental principle of English law that no person or body should be permitted to exceed its lawful powers. The starting point for judicial review of administrative action therefore is the doctrine of ultra vires, founded upon the doctrine of parliamentary sovereignty. Administrative authorities must be restrained from exceeding their powers and inferior tribunals must be prevented from exceeding the limits of their jurisdiction.

Ultra vires may be classified as being either substantive or procedural. Substantive ultra vires occurs where an administrative authority acts in excess of its statutory powers or in excess of its jurisdiction. As regards excess of power, it is the role of the court, by examining the parent Act, to determine the extent of the specific powers conferred upon the administrative authority by Parliament and ensure that those powers are not exceeded, an example being the case of *Attorney-General* v *Fulham Corporation* (1921). As for excess of jurisdiction, all administrative authorities have limited jurisdictions. Where an authority acts in excess of its jurisdiction as laid down in the parent Act, its acts will be ultra vires and void.

Procedural ultra vires occurs where a statute not only creates a body to perform some task on behalf of the Executive but in so doing also lays down a procedure that the body should follow in performing its functions. Where a procedural requirement is laid down in the parent Act, for example consultation with interested parties or the giving of notice, failure on the part of the administrative authority to follow that described procedure may, depending upon the nature of the requirement, result in its decision being ultra vires.

The second ground for judicial review envisaged by Lord Diplock, that of 'irrationality', applies in his Lordship's view to a decision which is so outrageous in its defiance of logic or of accepted moral standards that no sensible person who had applied his mind to the question to be decided could have arrived at it. It is of course implied by the courts as a matter of statutory construction that Parliament did not intend the powers it has conferred upon an administrative authority to be abused. In particular the courts will always imply that Parliament did not intend the administrative authority to act unreasonably and will, therefore, render unreasonable administrative action ultra vires. However, unreasonableness is a subjective concept and opinions can vary as to whether a particular decision is reasonable or not. Judicial review is concerned with the legality of decisions not their merits. The courts therefore have given the word 'unreasonable' a somewhat specialised meaning in the context of administrative law. According to Lord Greene MR in the case of *Associated Provincial Picture Houses Ltd* v *Wednesbury Corporation* (1948) a decision may be ultra vires if it can be proved to be unreasonable in the sense that the court considers it to be a decision which no reasonable body could take.

He said that a decision would be unreasonable if it failed to observe certain principles. A person entrusted with a discretion must direct himself properly in law. He must call his attention to the matters which he is bound to consider. Finally he must exclude from his consideration matters which are irrelevant to what he has to consider.

A growing number of decisions seem to illustrate that the courts are now willing to invalidate administrative action on the grounds that there is an absence of evidence to justify it. Also if a power is granted to an administrative authority for one purpose, it cannot be used to fulfil another purpose, the case of *Congreve* v *Home Office* (1976) being an example. The failure to exercise a discretionary power will also be ground for review. If an administrative authority upon which a power has been conferred delegates the right to exercise that power to another body, or fetters itself in the free exercise of that power, then its actions will be construed by the court as ultra vires and void. Fraud or bad faith will also render a decision open to review.

Lord Diplock described his third head on which administrative action is subject to control by judicial review as 'procedural impropriety'. His Lordship includes in this not only the failure to observe basic rules of natural justice but also the failure by an administrative tribunal to observe procedural rules that are expressly laid down in the legislative instrument by which its jurisdiction is conferred.

The rule that certain powers must be exercised in accordance with natural justice is one of the most important principles of judicial review of administrative action. The traditional view of natural justice is that it comprises two procedural rules. Firstly the rule that no man is to be condemned without a hearing. A person is entitled to notice of the case he has to meet and must be afforded a fair opportunity to answer the case against him and to present his own cause. People affected by judicial and administrative decisions have a right that the decision-maker should be impartial. Natural justice will therefore be breached where the person taking a decision has an interest in the case or where the person taking the decision is biased. Recently a third limb of natural justice has appeared, the so-called duty to act fairly. In many respects this duty encompasses both of the traditional rules, but it may possibly apply to a wider range of decisions. The precise requirements of natural justice will vary with the circumstances of each case, such as the nature of the decision being taken, the status and interest of the applicant, etc.

Type 3: An essay involving discussion of all aspects of judicial review of administrative action.

QUESTION 4

'Judicial review is concerned, not with the decisions, but with the decision making process'. (*Chief Constable of North Wales Police* v *Evans* [1982] 1 WLR 1155 per Lord Brightman 1174).

Discuss.

University of London LLB Examination
(for External Students) Constitutional Law June 1985 Q6

Skeleton solution

• Introduction: nature of administrative law; purpose of judicial review.

• The distinction between an appeal and judicial review.

• Examples to illustrate that judicial review is concerned with the decision making process: ultra vires - substantive and procedural; natural justice - procedural nature of audi alteram partem and nemo judex in causa sua.

• Public law remedies as an illustration of judicial review being concerned with the decision making process: the effect of an order of certiorari.

• Conclusion.

Suggested solution

Administrative law is the law relating to the control of governmental power, and in particular the legal controls upon the exercise of those powers by subordinate administrative authorities. Judicial review is the means whereby the courts achieve this control, and as Lord Brightman points out, in reviewing administrative action the court is not so much concerned with the merits of an actual decision, but rather with the process by which that decision was reached.

Judicial review must, therefore, be distinguished from an appeal. An appeal is concerned with the merits of a decision. A superior court is thus called upon to determine whether the decision of a lower court is right or wrong. With judicial review, however, the Divisional Court of the Queen's Bench Division is called upon to consider the legality of an act or order of a subordinate body. It must determine whether that act or order is lawful or unlawful. Instead of substituting its own decision for that of some other body, as on appeal, the court on review is concerned only with the question whether the act or order under attack should be allowed to stand or not.

The grounds upon which judicial review will lie illustrate the fact that it is the decision making process rather than the actual decision which is the subject of the review. Ultra vires, for example, is based upon the fundamental principle of English law that no person or body should be permitted to exceed its lawful powers. When considering the question of ultra vires therefore the courts are not concerned with the merits of a particular decision, but rather with discovering whether or not the administrative authority in question has acted in excess of its statutory powers (see for example *Attorney-General* v *Fulham Corporation* (1921)) or acted in excess of its jurisdiction (*Anisminic* v *Foreign Compensation Commission* (1969)), or whether or not the authority in the performance of its functions has followed the procedures prescribed by the parent Act: eg *Grunwick Processing Laboratories Ltd* v *ACAS* (1978)). The point is illustrated by the power of the court to declare an excess of jurisdiction on the part of an administrative authority to be ultra vires. All administrative authorities have limited jurisdiction. Where an authority acts in excess of its jurisdiction as laid down in the parent Act, its acts will be ultra vires and void. But where an authority makes a mistake, the traditional view (*R* v *Fulham, Hammersmith and Kensington Rent Tribunal ex parte Zerek* (1951)) has been that so long as the authority is acting within its jurisdiction to hear an applicant, it does not lose its jurisdiction and thereby act ultra vires, by coming to a wrong conclusion, whether it was wrong in law or in fact. Therefore the fact that an administrative authority makes a mistake in the exercise of a power does not necessarily render its decision ultra vires, and thereby subject to judicial review, so long as the error was committed within its jurisdiction.

Similarly with procedural ultra vires, when, for example, the courts are determining whether or not there has been an unreasonable use of a discretion the courts are concerned with the legality of the process by which the discretion was exercised and not with its merits. The requirements of reasonableness summarised by Lord Greene in *Associated Provincial Picture Houses Ltd* v *Wednesbury Corporation* (1948) illustrate this by being wholly and exclusively concerned with the decision making process viz has the person entrusted with a discretion directed himself properly in law, called to his attention those matters which he is bound to consider and excluded from his consideration matters which are irrelevant. So long as these procedural requirements have been satisfied the decision reached will stand and will not be subject to review.

The requirements of natural justice also illustrate the point that judicial review is concerned solely with the decision making process. The right to a fair hearing, audi alteram partem, in practice means that a person or body taking a decision must consider both sides of the case before taking that decision. No man is to be condemned without a hearing. Where a decision is one to which natural justice applies, or where the decision involves the duty to act fairly, then the person or body taking that decision must observe certain procedural requirements: see *Selvarajan* v *Race Relations Board* (1976). Basically, the right to a fair hearing requires that a person who stands to be affected by the decision of an administrative authority should be given notice of the case he has to meet and a fair opportunity to answer the case against him and to present his own side of the case. The risk against bias, nemo judex in causa sua, is also purely procedural in providing that no man should be a judge in his own cause (*Dimes* v *Grand Junction Canal Proprietors* (1852); *Metropolitan Properties Ltd* v *Lannon* (1969)) ie justice must be seen to be done.

The public law remedies available under an application for judicial review also illustrate the fact that judicial review is concerned not with the decisions but with the decision making process. The effect of an order of certiorari for example is to quash the decision of an inferior body, thus rendering it null and void. However, in quashing a decision by way of certiorari the reviewing court does not substitute its own decision for that of the inferior body, but usually simply refers the case back to the authority concerned to decide against this time observing the rules of natural justice or acting intra vires.

The aim of judicial review therefore is to ensure that public bodies act within the law. It is not aimed at compensating the individual for what he has lost because of the ultra vires in question: *Dunlop* v *Woollahra Municipal Council* (1981). Consequently the courts are only concerned with the legality of a decision, not with its merits. The court is not there to substitute its own value judgments for those of the inferior body. Judicial review must therefore be contrasted with a statutory right of appeal where a decision can be overruled and a new decision taken on the merits of the case. With judicial review a decision may simply be quashed and remitted to the inferior body to take again. By exercising their powers of judicial review the courts hope to indicate to administrative bodies the way in which they should act in future, and through this the courts can provide fairer and more efficient administrative practices.

Type 4: An essay on one topic within judicial review - exclusion of judicial review.

QUESTION 5

Assume that the Supplementary Benefits Bill is as follows:

'The decision of the Supplementary Benefits Commission shall be final and conclusive and no decision or purported decision of the Commission shall be questioned or reviewed by any court by injunction, declaratory judgment or application for review.'

Advise the parliamentary draftsman whether this would be effective to preclude challenge for any administrative law error and further advise on any improvements that could be made to the drafting of this provision.

University of London LLB Examination
(for External Students) Constitutional Law June 1984 Q7

Skeleton solution

- Introduction - statement of the general position adopted by the courts where their powers of judicial review are apparently excluded by statute.
- Effect of a finality clause.
- Effect of a 'shall not be questioned' clause - the *Anisminic* decision.
- Conclusion - need to include very wide exclusion formula.

Suggested solution

Various formulae have been inserted into legislation with the intention of precluding judicial intervention, but it is by no means the case that this will be achieved. The courts are most unwilling to relinquish their powers of judicial review and will only do so if a statute contains very clear words.

The Supplementary Benefits Bill contains several clauses to oust or restrict the courts' jurisdiction. First of all it provides that 'The decision of the Supplementary Benefits Commission shall be final ...'. The courts have not been impressed by such 'finality' clauses, holding that they only protect decisions made on facts and not law. Jurisdiction defects are not rendered immune by such a clause, nor are errors on the face of the record. In *R v Medical Appeal Tribunal ex parte Gilmore* (1957) it was held that the decision of the Tribunal was open to attack despite the existence of a finality clause. Denning LJ reviewed the authorities and concluded that the only effect of the clause was to prevent an appeal: judicial review, whether for jurisdictional error or error on the face of the record, remained unimpaired. Even this limited effect has been subsequently diminished. In *Tehrani v Rostron* (1971) the Court of Appeal held that, despite the existence of finality provisions it was still possible to state a case, at least where declarations of certiorari would themselves have been available.

The finality clause contained in the Bill is therefore, on its own, probably of little effect. However, the Bill goes on to say ' ... no decision or purported decision of the commission shall be questioned or reviewed by any court, by injunction, declaratory judgment or application for review'. The Bill therefore contains, in addition to the finality clause, a 'shall not be questioned' clause in conjunction with a series of restrictions akin to a 'no certiorari' clause.

Regarding the 'shall not be questioned' clause in the *Anisminic* case (1969) s4(4) of the Foreign Compensation Act 1950 stated that a determination of the commission shall not be called in question in any court of law. The House of Lords unanimously held that this only protected determinations which were intra vires: ultra vires determinations were not determinations at all. They were nullities which could be of no effect. *Anisminic* therefore establishes the basic principle that if an authority or tribunal exceeds its jurisdiction then its decision is regarded by the courts as invalid and beyond the protection of any exclusionary formula yet devised by Parliamentary draftsmen. However, the Bill refers to 'decisions or purported decisions'. Does the reference to purported decisions effectively oust the courts' jurisdiction to review ultra vires decisions of the commission? It is very doubtful that such is the case. The courts have consistently held that errors in excess of jurisdiction are reviewable and in line with the strict construction placed by the courts on such clauses, the clause will probably be ineffective.

The Supplementary Benefits Bill also contains a series of exclusion clauses seeking to exclude review by a court by injunction, declaratory judgment or application for review. While exclusion of particular remedies may be effective in certain cases the exclusion of review, or 'no certiorari' clauses have been strictly interpreted by the courts, who are reluctant to see their powers of judicial review diminished. Such clauses do not affect the courts' power to review jurisdictional defects and in that respect are ineffective, but such a clause can exclude review for error on the face of the record.

In *South East Asia Firebricks Sdn Bhd* v *Non-Metallic Mineral Products Manufacturing Employees Union* (1981) the Malaysian Industrial Relations Act 1967 contained a finality clause, a shall not be challenged or questioned section, and a term providing that awards of the industrial court should not be quashed. The Privy Council held that the finality clause was of no effect, but that the provision that an award should not be quashed was effective, and certainly this, together with the words 'shall not be called in question in any court of law' were wide enough to cover certiorari. But only errors of law within the jurisdiction were immune from attack. A jurisdictional error could still be impugned.

Therefore the clause in the Bill purporting to oust the courts' power of review will be ineffective in respect of jurisdictional errors by the commission and may even be ineffective as regards errors of law within the jurisdiction of the commission. However, while the authorities show that review of jurisdictional error may never be ousted, it is possible to oust the courts' jurisdiction in respect of error of law within the jurisdiction of the commission providing that there is a clear and express exclusion formula in the governing statute. It may therefore improve the effectiveness of the clause in the Supplementary Benefit Bill if the draftsmen were to adopt a *South East Asia Firebricks* 'omnibus' type of exclusion providing that decisions of the commission are 'final and conclusive, and no decision shall be challenged, appealed against, reviewed, quashed or called in question in any court of law.'

12 LOCAL GOVERNMENT

12.1 Introduction

12.2 Key points

12.3 Recent cases and statutes

12.4 Analysis of questions

12.5 Question

12.1 Introduction

This area may came up as a separate examination area, but it will often be part of a judicial review question. If it does appear it will be in an essay question.

12.2 Key points

a) *Structure*

Prior to 1 April 1986

i) London - London Government Act 1963

- Greater London Council (central coordinating body).
- 32 London Boroughs (and City of London Corporation).

ii) England and Wales - Local Government Act 1972

- England: 6 metropolitan county councils; 36 metropolitan districts; parish councils.
- 39 county councils; 296 district councils; parish councils.
- Wales: 8 county councils; 37 district councils; community councils.
- more centralised in the non-metropolitan countries.

b) *Recent reforms*

i) Local Government Act 1985

- Abolished central bodies - ie GLC and 6 metropolitan county councils.
- Functions of GLC and metropolitan county councils taken over initially by non-elected bodies - ultimately to be transferred to boroughs and districts.

ii) Reasons for reform

- Two-tier system not necessary - most functions already carried out at local level.
- Money saved.
- Political legislation to dispense with opposition.

c)   *Internal organisation*

   i)   Members

- County council: 60-100; elected every four years.

      Metropolitan district council 50-80; 1/3 retire each year.

      Non-metropolitan district council: 30-60; one of above systems for election.

- London - elections every three years.

   ii)   Meetings

- Section 101 LGA 1972: widespread delegation to committees.

- Public Bodies (Admission to Meetings) Act 1960 - public and press entitled to be present at council and committee meetings unless authority passes resolution to exclude them in the public interest: *R* v *Brent Health Authority ex parte Francis* [1985] QB 869.

d)   *Sources of income*

   i)   Community charge

- Personal community charge is a tax on all adults.

- Standard community charge is to be paid by the owner of a house or flat where no-one is registered as solely or mainly resident.

- Collective community charge deals with hostels for example where people only stay for short periods. The owners will be liable.

- Uniform business rate

   ii)   Grants from central government

- specific eg police, student grants, urbanisation.

- general 'revenue support grant'.

   iii)   Borrowing

   iv)   Charges for provision of services and facilities

e)   *Powers of local authorities*

   i)   Dependent on Parliament (via statute) for their powers; subject to doctrine of ultra vires.

   ii)   Power involves exercise of discretion - must be exercised 'reasonably', 'bona fide'.

   iii)   Statutory corporations - can sue and be sued.

iv) Legislation

- Promote private bills.

- By-laws - subject to central government approval and ultra vires: *Kruse* v *Johnson* [1898] 2 QB 91.

f) *Reforms of control over local authorities*

i) By central government

- Enabling statutes.

- By-laws, borrowing, capital expenditure - subject to approval.

- Co-operation/consultation.

- Grants - general and specific - recently brought under great control.

- Default powers: minister may intervene where authority failing properly to exercise power: *R* v *Secretary of State for Environment ex parte Norwich City Council* [1982] QB 808.

ii) By the courts - doctrine of ultra vires

- Local Authority must not act unreasonably: 'Wednesbury Principle'; *Secretary of State for Education and Science* v *Tameside Metropolitan Borough Council* [1977] AC 1014.

- Negligence: *Anns* v *Merton London Borough Council* [1978] AC 728 - vicarious liability for torts of servants.

iii) Extra-judicial

- Local commissioners hear complaints concerning maladministration by local authorities.

- Local authority accounts audited annually by district auditors.

12.3 Recent cases and statutes

Local Government Finance Act 1988

12.4 Analysis of questions

Questions specifically on local government are not favoured. However, there may appear a question on the relationship between local government and central government and students will need to know the structure and powers of local government. A more common question will be to examine the student's knowledge of the ways in which the courts control the exercise of local authority powers through the doctrine of ultra vires. Many cases of judicial review involve local authorities.

12.5 Question

One of the most difficult constitutional problems today is striking a balance between central government control and local government autonomy. Discuss.

University of London LLB Examination
(for External Students) Constitutional Law June 1987 Q5

General comment

A very topical question concerning the conflict between central and local democracy.

Skeleton solution

• Introduction. Unitary nature of the United Kingdom; the role of local government.

• Central government control of local authorities. Finance; regulations; inspection; default powers; abolition.

▪ The reasons for conflict. Maintenance of national standards; national economic policy.

• Relationship between central and local government. Partnership or central dominance; problem of conflict of democracies.

Suggested solution

Although the United Kingdom is a unitary state there is a highly developed system of local government. The organs of local government serve two broad purposes. Firstly, they enable many public services to be administered at a level nearer the people for the benefit of whom the service is provided. Secondly, they enable local political opinion to be organised and expressed. Local authorities, however, although representative bodies chosen by popular election, have not the autonomy of Parliament; indeed they are dependent upon Parliament for their powers.

The powers of local authorities derive either expressly or by implication from statute and they are exercised subject to the doctrine of ultra vires. The application of these rules in disputed cases is a matter for the courts and no local authority can determine the extent of its own powers. But within the limits of its powers, and subject to the performance of any statutory duties laid upon it, a local authority has a discretion in deciding how it is to administer the services for which it is responsible. In practice however this discretion is subject to many forms of direct and indirect pressure from central government and especially recently there has developed an increasing tendency for central government to restrict the freedom of local authorities to decide their own policies.

The array of local authority controls available to central government is formidable. Perhaps some of the most effective are those concerned with local authority finance. The services provided by local government will of course require expenditure and the two main sources of local authority finance to meet this expenditure are the community charge and grants from central government. But central government departments not only have the power to make grants but also to withhold them. They also have the power to control borrowing for capital projects. Most important today however, is 'community charge capping' whereby central government may set the maximum rate in the pound to be levied in any one year by any local authority designated by the Secretary of State.

As well as these powers over local authority finance, central government departments also have powers to prescribe rules for the conduct of local services. This may be achieved directly by regulations, or indirectly by the introduction of parliamentary legislation. Certain services, for example the police and education, are subject to central government inspection. Relevant central government departments also have the power to confirm or refuse to confirm by-laws, compulsory purchase orders, educational schemes, senior appointments etc, to conduct local inquiries under certain statutory powers and to entertain appeals in respect of certain local authority decisions, for example refusals of planning permission. Central government departments may also exercise default powers, by removing responsibility for the conduct of a service from one authority to another or by taking over responsibility for the service centrally or by issuing a mandatory order or obtaining from the courts an order of mandamus to compel the authority to carry out its statutory duties.

By its very nature therefore local government implies a measure of local self government. Local authorities do not operate as mere agents of central departments subject to the latter's full direction and control. But, because of central government's responsibility for national policies some of which, for example education and housing, depend completely upon local implementation, it is inevitable that claims have to be made by central government departments to supervise or control local authority activities, both for the overall maintenance of standards of service and reasons of national economic policy.

This relationship which results from these claims of central government and from the desire of local authorities for some autonomy is sometimes described as a partnership. However in reality it is central government that dominates the relationship. This is inevitable. Increasingly party politics is infiltrating local government and where the political composition of a local authority differs from that of the central government there is great scope for conflict. Local authorities are now responsible for the exercise of many powers and duties and spend vast sums of public money. They can therefore seriously frustrate the plans of the central government. But in any conflict it is usually the central government that wins. Central government controls Parliament and Parliament is supreme. Legislation may be enacted to control the functions of local authorities or even abolish authorities in some cases. Local authorities must not stand in the way of central government policy. But the problem is of course that local authorities are elected just as central government is elected and they too have their mandate. The great problem is striking a balance between these two conflicts of democracy.

13 THE EUROPEAN CONVENTION AND A BILL OF RIGHTS

13.1 Introduction

13.2 Key points

13.3 Recent cases and statutes

13.4 Analysis of questions

13.5 Questions

13.1 Introduction

The civil liberties we enjoy in the United Kingdom are described as residual. That is to say we are free to do what we like as long as it is not against the law. This position can be contrasted with the position in countries with a written Constitution where individual freedoms are usually defined and protected in a 'Bill of Rights'.

Legislation which curtails freedom includes, for example, public order legislation, laws on obscenity, laws to protect national security and so on. By the same token some legislation confers rights eg race relations and sex equality.

Traditionally the courts have viewed their role as being to protect liberty. Note, however, that under the doctrine of parliamentary sovereignty the government is often able to pass legislation which cannot be challenged by the courts and some pressure groups - eg the National Council for Civil Liberties - see significant inroads being made into our traditional freedoms.

13.2 Key points

a) *Why do we need a Bill of Rights?*

  i) The common law is inadequate to protect human rights; it lays down negative as opposed to positive rights. For example there is no positive right to freedom of speech but merely a number of rules about what cannot be said ie defamation, obscenity etc.

  ii) Whilst rights are given to the individual by the common law and statute an individual would have to search through a host of cases and statutory provisions to find out what his civil rights were; much better for such rights to be contained in one document which would be enshrined in Englishmen's minds much as basic rights contained in the American Constitution are known by all United States citizens.

  iii) There is no written Constitution. In countries with such a written Constitution the courts are free to strike down legislation which is in breach of the Constitution. In the United Kingdom the concept of parliamentary sovereignty means that Parliament can do no wrong; so long as an Act receives the approval of both Houses of Parliament and the assent of the monarch the courts are bound to apply it even if it does interfere with what elsewhere would be basic civil liberties: *Pickin* v *British Railways Board* [1974] AC 765.

iv) The inability of the courts to control Parliament has become increasingly important in the light of the fact that government cannot be kept in check by Parliament. The government of the day by reason of the majority vote system in Parliament can force any measure through the House of Commons and the House of Lords can only delay legislation, it cannot veto it.

v) Whilst the United Kingdom is a signatory to the European Convention on Human Rights (1953) it has no binding effect in the United Kingdom and, furthermore, on a number of occasions the United Kingdom has been found to be in breach of the Convention, eg telephone tapping by police in *Malone* v *Metropolitan Police Commissioner* [1979] Ch 344.

b) *Should we simply adopt the European Convention or produce a completely new document?*

The government has indicated that its preferred view is to simply adopt the European Convention. To do otherwise would mean that there would be two documents guaranteeing basic civil liberties, one English and one European. There would be a danger of conflict, contradiction and confusion. However there are arguments against this approach as follows:

i) The European Convention is almost 40 years old. It was mooted and designed in the years immediately following the end of the second World War. Can it really be said to be relevant to what is today a very different world?

ii) It is drafted in very general terms; our judges are used to specifically worded statutes which they can and do interpret literally. Would our judges be able to deal with such generally worded provisions which would require more than a mere literal interpretation? And if they were so able would they be accused of making law and thereby come into conflict with the legislature?

iii) The Convention itself is not ideal. For example the right to 'liberty and security of the person' (Article 5) is expressly subject to a number of exceptions allowing, for example, the lawful detention of persons for the prevention of infectious diseases, of persons of unsound mind, of alcoholics, of vagrants and of drug addicts. Article 11 which protects the 'right of freedom of assembly' etc is subject to restrictions - in particular governments can argue 'national security' as a legitimate reason for denying such a freedom. Finally Article 15 allows a government 'in time of war or other public emergency' to ignore certain of the Convention's provisions. What is a 'public emergency' can be a very subjective matter!

iv) Furthermore, some of the Convention's ideals may be against popular political thinking at any given time. For example the right to 'peaceful enjoyment of possessions' would seem to militate against public taxation.

Perhaps the answer would be to adopt the European Convention but with amendments to bring it in line with modern requirements.

c) *How could any Bill of Rights Act be 'entrenched'?*

i) The problem

Generally Parliament cannot bind its successors. Accordingly it cannot pass 'unrepealable' Acts. See: *Vauxhall Estates* v *Liverpool Corporation* [1932] 1 KB 733 and *Ellen Street Estates* v *Minister of Health* [1934] 1 KB 590.

Thus in theory it would be impossible to pass a Bill of Rights which could be 'entrenched' for evermore.

ii) The answer

However, there are many statutes that could not, in practice, be repealed eg Commonwealth of Australia Act 1901, Act of Union with Scotland Act 1706, European Communities Act 1972.

Surely a Bill of Rights Act could not in fact be repealed? Would such a repealing Act get the Royal Assent and, if it did, would the courts be prepared to obey such a repealing statute?

13.3 Recent cases and statutes

There have not been any recent cases or legislation of particular significance in this area; the important ones are mentioned in section 13.2 Key points (above).

Students must be able to cite the civil liberties preserved by the major Articles of the European Convention on Human Rights. To show why the United Kingdom needs a Bill of Rights reference to cases from the chapters on parliamentary sovereignty, public order and freedom of expression (chapters 3, 4, 14 and 15) will also be required.

13.4 Analysis of questions

The question of whether the United Kingdom should pass its own Bill of Rights is one that has been raised periodically by various pressure groups over the last two decades. Its appearance as a question on the examination paper has very much corresponded with years in which the cry for the introduction of a Bill of Rights has been louder than usual. Any European agreement on a Social Charter is likely to result in renewed cries for the introduction of such a Bill and, accordingly, you can expect a question on this area over the next few years. Any such question will be in the form of an essay requiring the candidate to talk about the following:

a) The need for, and effect of, a Bill of Rights.

b) Whether such a Bill should simply incorporate the European Convention on Human Rights or should the United Kingdom adopt a completely new document.

c) How, if at all, it could be ensured that any Bill of Rights Act passed is not repealed in the future.

13.5 Questions

QUESTION 1

Argue the case for and against the adoption of the European Convention on Human Rights and its protocols as a Bill of Rights for the United Kingdom.

University of London LLB Examination
(for External Students) Constitutional Law June 1986 Q9

General comment

This question requires a good knowledge of the arguments for and against the adoption of the European Convention on Human Rights as a Bill of Rights. A knowledge of Lord Wade's Bill to incorporate the Convention into United Kingdom domestic law would also be useful.

Skeleton solution

* Introduction: the existing constitutional safeguards for protecting human rights in the United Kingdom.

* The European Convention on Human Rights: the objects of the Convention and the machinery for enforcement.

* The arguments in favour of adopting the Convention as a Bill of Rights for the United Kingdom.

* The arguments against adopting the Convention: the problem of parliamentary sovereignty; politicising the judiciary.

* Lord Wade's Bill to incorporate the Convention into domestic law.

Suggested solution

The United Kingdom Constitution is unwritten in the formal sense and accordingly lays great emphasis on the virtues of the common law and the legislative supremacy of Parliament. It relies heavily on the political process to ensure that Parliament does not override the basic rights and liberties of the subject, nor remove from the courts the adjudication of disputes between the citizen and the state arising out of the exercise of executive power.

This traditional British approach to individual liberties is considered by many to be outdated and incapable of protecting individual rights from executive encroachment. The critics advocate the creation of a new Bill of Rights for the United Kingdom. Accordingly, in 1978 a select committee of the House of Lords was established to consider whether a Bill of Rights was desirable and, if so, what form it should take. The committee, while doubting that a Bill of Rights was desirable, nevertheless held unanimously that if there were to be a Bill of Rights, it should be a Bill to incorporate the European Convention of Human Rights into United Kingdom law.

The European Convention on Human Rights (see: Beddard, *Human Rights and Europe*, 2nd ed, 1980), prepared under the auspices of the Council of Europe, entered into force in September 1953. The Convention is a treaty under international law and

131

its authority derives solely from the consent of those states who have become parties to it. The Convention declares certain human rights which should be protected by law in each state and provides political and judicial procedures by which alleged infringements of these rights may be examined at an international level. Every state party to the Convention has a duty to ensure that its domestic law conforms to the Convention, but a state is under no duty to incorporate the Convention itself within its domestic law. While about half the states who are parties to the Convention have incorporated it within their domestic law, others, including the United Kingdom, have not incorporated the Convention. Successive British governments have maintained that human rights are already adequately protected by law in the United Kingdom.

Those who argue in favour of adopting the European Convention as a Bill of Rights for the United Kingdom point out that human rights are not adequately protected under our present law and that further constitutional protection for human rights is therefore necessary. In support of their case they point to the ever increasing role of the state in economic and social affairs and the widespread public disillusionment with the parliamentary process and the 'undemocratic' electoral system which produces a legislature dominated and controlled by the executive. There is also concern at the record of the United Kingdom under the European Convention on Human Rights and dissatisfaction with the performance of the courts in dealing with disputes between the citizen and the state. With the executive every day assuming more statutory powers and in so doing eroding our common law liberties, so it becomes more vital to provide safeguards against the abuse of those powers.

Assuming that some form of Bill of Rights is needed in the United Kingdom, incorporation of the European Convention would probably be the easiest and most acceptable option available to the government. There is no dispute as to the rights protected. The Convention very wisely omits economic and social rights, over which considerable political controversy might arise, and is confined to certain basic rights and liberties which the framers of the Convention considered would be generally accepted in the liberal democracies of Western Europe. Incorporation of the Convention would also avoid the frequent humiliation suffered by the United Kingdom government before the European Court of Human Rights when, in the glare of international publicity, it is found in breach of its international obligations under the Convention. These foreign 'judges' would no longer be able to interfere with our law and instead breaches of the convention would be dealt with before our own municipal courts.

However, to be fully effective incorporation would have to enable the British courts to apply the Convention if necessary in preference to existing rules of statute or common law and this will entail grafting onto the present Constitution an added power in the courts to give redress to the individual even against an Act of Parliament. Such an attempt would raise issues concerning the relationship of the courts to the political process, including the special difficulties inherent in the attempt by a supreme Parliament to bind itself.

There are therefore formidable legal and political problems in the incorporation of the European Convention as a new Bill of Rights for the United Kingdom (see: Jaconelli,

Enacting a Bill of Rights, the Legal Problems, 1980). It is extremely difficult to bring about any enactment of fundamental rights that may not be violated by ordinary process of legislation, and what is the value in having a Bill of Rights that cannot bind future Parliaments? Also, is it desirable to have constitutional change likely to give greater power to the judiciary? Some argue that, in reviewing administrative decisions, the courts are already inclined to interfere in political disputes and should not be encouraged to extend this to the review of legislative decisions: political decisions should be made by democratically elected politicians, not by judges.

The House of Lords in 1979 did in fact approve a Bill proposed by the Liberal peer Lord Wade, that sought to incorporate the European Convention in United Kingdom law and provide a compromise which both enabled the United Kingdom to give better effect to its existing obligations under the Convention, and respond positively to the domestic movement for the greater protection of human rights. However the Bill failed to receive government support in the House of Commons. It remains to be seen therefore whether future decisions of the European Court of Human Rights will influence government thinking in favour of incorporating the Convention.

QUESTION 2

What differences, if any, would incorporation of the European Convention on Human Rights into British law make to the British Constitution?

University of London LLB Examination
(for External Students) Constitutional Law June 1987 Q9

General comment

Although this question is phrased rather generally students should concentrate on the effects of incorporation on the sovereignty of Parliament and the role of the judiciary in interpreting and enforcing a Bill of Rights in the United Kingdom.

Skeleton solution

• Introduction. The need for a Bill of Rights.

• Mechanism for incorporation of the European Convention on Human Rights into United Kingdom law.

• Effects of incorporation on the Constitution. The sovereignty of Parliament; the role of the judiciary.

Suggested solution

Recently there have been increasing demands for the enactment of a Bill of Rights in the United Kingdom to safeguard the fundamental rights and freedoms of the individual. As the executive becomes more powerful, controlling the legislature and interfering more and more in the lives of the citizen, some protection, it is argued, becomes necessary. The State has become prosecutor and judge in its own cause. Because of this the common law negative freedoms we enjoy are under constant attack and the judges are powerless to check the legislative supremacy of that agent of the executive, Parliament. In most countries there is a written Constitution which is not

133

just a sacred piece of paper but a statement that the people are the ultimate source of power, that the state and its legislature and its civil servants and laws are the servants of the people. It is argued that the enactment of a Bill of Rights in the United Kingdom will help to reassert the supremacy of the individual over the state.

To achieve this the simplest and perhaps most obvious answer is to look to the European Convention on Human Rights. The United Kingdom is a party to the Convention and successive British governments both socialist and conservative have allowed citizens to petition the European Commission of Human Rights and seek enforcement of the rights and freedoms set out in the Convention in international law. Why not go one step further and incorporate the European Convention into domestic law so that its provisions may be enforced and applied by British judges in British courts? But if such incorporation did take place would it make any difference to the operation of the British constitution as regards the protection of fundamental rights and freedoms? Probably not.

This is because the enactment of a Bill of Rights in the United Kingdom involves the consideration of a theoretically insurmountable problem, the sovereignty of Parliament. A Bill of Rights is a piece of paper. It has no practical value unless it can be enforced against those having the power to take away the rights and freedoms of the citizen. But the United Kingdom Parliament is sovereign. There are no legal restraints on its legislative powers. This absence of legal restraint has three aspects: Parliament is legally competent to legislate upon any subject matter; no Parliament can bind its successors or be bound by its predecessors; and once Parliament has legislated no court or other person can pass judgment upon the validity of the legislation.

Parliament may therefore make or unmake any law. There is no area or subject matter outside the scope of its legislative powers. Parliament is also unable to limit its own legislative powers for the future. Parliament cannot bind its successors and a later Parliament is always, in theory at least, able to expressly repeal the legislation made by an earlier Parliament. Also, under the doctrine of implied repeal as expressed in *Vauxhall Estates* v *Liverpool Corporation* (1932) the provisions of an earlier Act can always be repealed by implication by provisions in a later Act which are inconsistent with those in the earlier Act. Further, in *Ellen Street Estates Ltd* v *Minister of Health* (1934) it was also held that Parliament cannot, by a statement in an earlier Act, effectively provide that the provisions of that Act cannot be repealed by implication by inconsistent provisions in a later Act. The role of the courts is also limited with regard to Acts of Parliament. For example the case of *Pickin* v *British Railways Board* (1974) illustrates the point that once it is established that an Act has received the consent of the House of Commons, the assent of the House of Lords (or that it has been passed under the provisions of the Parliament Acts 1911-1949), and the assent of the Sovereign all the courts can do is apply it subject to their limited powers of statutory interpretation.

It can be seen therefore that even if the present Parliament enacts a Bill of Rights for the United Kingdom a later Parliament intent on restricting or abolishing the rights and freedoms contained in it may do so either by express enactment or even impliedly by the enactment of a later statute which conflicts with its provisions. The courts will be powerless to intervene. So long as Parliament remains sovereign there can be no entrenchment of legislation against future amendment or repeal. Only Parliament can limit its own sovereignty and such limitations must have been enacted in the form of statute. However no Parliament can bind its successors. Therefore whatever limitations are imposed upon the sovereignty of Parliament by one statute may be repealed by a subsequent Act. Therefore in theory at least it may be true to say that even if enacted, a Bill of Rights could be repealed tomorrow and the existence of the Bill will make no difference to this aspect of our Constitution.

However in theory there are means by which limitations can be placed upon the sovereignty of Parliament. For example some statutes such as the Statute of Westminster 1931 contain limitations as to the scope and subject matter of parliamentary legislation. Others such as the Colonial Laws Validity Act 1865 contain limitations as to the manner and form of future legislation. The real check upon the sovereignty of Parliament however in practice remains public opinion. The government always knows that it will have to face a General Election within a few years and this stark reality may have a restraining effect upon their legislative proposals and deter any attempted government tampering with the Bill of Rights. Of course these informal restraints are present and operating already to curtail executive power and in this respect the presence of a Bill of Rights will make little difference.

One difference that would be made to the British Constitution by the incorporation of the European Convention on Human Rights into British law concerns the role of the judiciary. A Bill of Rights would involve a shift of power from elected and accountable Members of Parliament to judges who are neither elected nor accountable. These judges will be involved not just in making interim policy choices about what the law should be, pending action by the Legislature, but in making final policy choices which some would argue they cannot be trusted to do. It will turn judges into legislators. Judges whose job it is to know and apply the law will be asked to create and form the law. In this respect it may be doubted that British court procedure is the best environment in which to thoroughly analyse the kind of problematic political questions such a Bill of Rights will raise.

QUESTION 3

A Bill of Rights has been proposed making it unlawful 'to discriminate on any grounds such as sex, race, colour, language, religion, political or other opinion, national and social origin, associated with a national minority, property or other statutus'.

Would such a Bill or Rights provide for the better protection of human rights in the United Kingdom?

University of London LLB Examination
(for External Students) Constitutional Law June 1981 Q9

Skeleton solution

Introduction identifying ways in which the United Kingdom specifically provides protection to areas such as race relations and sex equality, and the position of the European Convention in the United Kingdom. Problems with the Bill of Rights proposed:

• Entrenchment

• Interpretation

Conclusion.

Suggested solution

To discuss this point it is necessary first of all to briefly examine the ways that such rights are protected at present, and whether these are adequate in themselves. There is already in existence legislation against discrimination, for example, the Sex Discrimination Act 1975 and the Race Relations Act 1976, plus Habeas Corpus, but these exist more as a system of remedies rather than of rights. There is also the curious position that the UK is in as regards the European Convention of Human Rights. The UK signed the Convention and has ratified certain of the Protocols but has not incorporated the terms of the Convention into domestic law. The position at present therefore is that there is no right of action in the domestic courts - the only remedy for an individual citizen of the UK being to take a case to the European Commission against the Government for breaches of the Convention and ultimately to the European Court of Human Rights. In certain cases it appeared that the Convention might have a strong effect on British case law - in *R* v *Secretary of State for Home Dept ex parte Bhajan Singh* (1976) Lord Denning stated that immigration officers and the Secretary of State, in exercising their duties ought to bear in mind the principles stated in the Convention - however this statement was amended in a later case when he stated that immigration officials must go simply by immigration rules laid down by the Secretary of State. The present technical position appears to be that since the Convention is not part of the law it cannot be used otherwise than as a not very strong guide to statutory interpretation. It has been suggested that these safeguards are sufficient, but it may be argued that had a Bill of Rights been part of the UK Constitution it would not have been possible to pass recent Immigration Acts, nor to introduce the British Nationality Bill, all of which include an element of discrimination of the grounds of sex.

Looking at the Bill which has been proposed, there are a number of problems which need to be discussed; one of the main ones being the problem of entrenching such a Bill into the UK Constitution, for at present any Bill which is enacted can be easily repealed, either expressly or impliedly. Professor Hood Philips suggests the only way that such a Bill might be introduced would be to bring into being a 'New Parliament' which would owe its existence to a Constitution not enacted by itself, from which it would derive both its powers and limitations. There are alternatives to entrenchment which could be either to provide that a special majority in one or both houses is required for the repeal or amendment of any of the Bill's provisions or alternatively following Canada's lead and provide that in the case of conflict between past or future laws, and the Bill, that the Bill of Rights should override previous enactments, and imposing on the courts a presumption of interpretation excluding implied derogation by subsequent amendments.

A second problem equally important, would be the one concerning the interpretation of such a Bill. The law at present tends not to lay down general principles, but a Bill of this nature could not do anything else. Lord Gardiner puts this forward as his main argument against such a Bill - that as a mere declaration of principles the impact would be insignificant, and in addition judges would have an impossible task because of the inherent uncertainty. It has long been accepted under the UK Constitution that Parliament legislates in a specific form and that the role of the courts is to apply and interpret within narrow boundaries, that legislation. A Bill of Rights as suggested would be opening up a wide variety of legislative policies in a very general way and handing them over to the judiciary for detailed development. The House of Lords select committee which reported in 1978 on the question of incorporating the European Convention into the UK Constitution commented on this element of uncertainty, and on the amount of litigation that would be necessary in order not only to find the extent of the new rights, but also to check the validity of existing laws. All this leads to an obvious conclusion; a Bill of Rights is only as good as its interpreters, with the additional point that a Bill of Rights should represent the minimum standards; it has been suggested that if enacted it may be interpreted as indicating the maximum.

There now remains the point whether any alternatives to a Bill of this nature have been proposed rather than merely maintaining status quo. Firstly the 'piecemeal legislation' could be continued but the problem will still remain that it would only be a remedy - with the same situation of residual freedoms. Harry Street suggested that a Civil Rights Commission should be set up to codify and re-examine existing legislation and point towards proposals of a more positive declaration of rights. However this is likely to come up against similar problems as the existing Law Commission, that is, an inability to persuade the government to find legislative time for its proposals. It is suggested that a Civil Rights Commission would find governments even more unaccommodating since many of their proposals would contain a politically controversial element.

It seems apt to conclude with Michael Zander's remarks when he stated that the case for a Bill of Rights rests rather on the belief that it would make a distinct and valuable contribution to the better protection of human rights - though the extent is dependent on how it is regarded and interpreted by judges. It would give them a greater scope than exists in common law and statute and, he argues, that it would be grossly underestimating their ability to suggest that judges are not capable of adopting this broader and more wide ranging approach of interpretation.

QUESTION 4

Critically assess the following statement that 'the case for a Bill of Rights rests on the belief that it would make a distinct and valuable contribution to the better protection of human rights'.

University of London LLB Examination
(for External Students) Constitutional Law June 1988 Q6

General comment

The question seems to be inviting discussion on the issue of whether human rights are adequately protected by the British Constitution as it stands at present, or whether the enactment of specific legislation is called for. Thus some consideration of the protection offered under domestic legislation and the common law is called for. Thought should be given as to how an effective Bill of Rights might be introduced, and to the question of its contents.

Skeleton solution

Explain the protection offered under English law - statutory provisions - common law decision. Shortcomings of both - examples of breaches of human rights under the ECHR by the United Kingdom government. Problems of the contents of a Bill of Rights - problems of implementation.

Suggested solution

The question invites discussion of the merits and demerits of a Bill of Rights being enacted. One could commence by pointing out that there is already a Bill of Rights on the statute book, that of 1689, but of course that legislation was not concerned with the rights of individuals so much as the relationship between Parliament and the Crown. Whilst the Bill of 1689 may have been effective to prevent individuals being subject to arbitrary prerogative power as exercised by the monarch in person, it did little to protect the individual citizen from the excesses of governmental power exercised under the guise of parliamentary sovereignty; indeed one might well contend that one of the failings of the 'Glorious Revolution' was to place too much power in the hands of the legislature, and thereby the government.

There have been a number of attempts in recent years to introduce a Bill of Rights aimed at strengthening the protection of individual rights under English law. The most recent took the form of a Private Member's Bill introduced by Sir Edward Gardner, the Human Rights and Fundamental Freedoms Bill (1986), which sought to incorporate the European Convention on Human Rights into English law. The Bill very narrowly failed in the Commons*, but there was clearly considerable parliamentary support for such a measure.

The statement under consideration suggests that a Bill of Rights could make a distinct contribution to the better protection of human rights, thus prompting the question, distinct from what?

Under English law, individual rights are protected by either statute or common law. Examples of statutory protection are provided by the Race Relations Act 1976, Sex Discrimination Act 1975, and the Police and Criminal Evidence Act 1984. At common law decisions such as *Christie* v *Leachinsky* (1947), under which a police officer was required to inform a suspect of the grounds for an arrest, or *Entick* v *Carrington* (1765) under which the courts invalidated the practice of issuing general search warrants, have undoubtedly contributed to the protection of individual rights and liberties. Can it be said that this combined protection is so inadequate that a formal Bill of Rights is needed?

The problem with 'equal rights' or 'civil liberties' legislation is that such measures are always at the mercy of successive Parliaments. As a consequence of parliamentary sovereignty they can always be amended or repealed. Further, it can be argued that when Parliament places individual liberties on a statutory basis it can draft them in terms that make them more limited in operation than they were at common law. More generally, successive

Parliaments have fought shy of granting United Kingdom citizens positive statutory rights, such as the right to free expression, the right to information, and the right to privacy.

The failings of the common law are that it is sporadic in nature. The judiciary can only develop individual rights at common law if cases are brought before them. Whether or not this occurs is a haphazard affair, not the best way in which to tackle such a serious matter. In any event, any decision of the courts can be nullified by subsequent parliamentary action in the form of new legislation, which can even be retrospective if necessary. The courts have not always responded when called upon by litigants to defend or develop human rights. Mr Malone's arguments for a right to privacy fell upon deaf ears in *Malone* v *Metropolitan Police Commissioner* (1979), the Vice-Chancellor concluding that as there was no English law governing the matter of telephone tapping, he would be usurping the function of Parliament by holding that such action did amount to an invasion of the plaintiff's right to privacy regarding his communications.

On the basis of the above, Lord Scarman, amongst others, has contended (*The Guardian* 14 November 1988) that a Bill of Rights is needed in the British Constitution because individual rights are not adequately protected at present by statute and common law. Those who contend that human rights are not violated by the United Kingdom can be referred to the succession of findings against the United Kingdom by the European Court of Human Rights under the European Convention.

Matters in relation to which the British government, and by implication the British Constitution, has been found wanting are: the law of contempt; the law relating to telephone tapping; the rights of prisoners to communicate with lawyers; the rights of prisoners to be legally represented in prison disciplinary proceedings; detention without trial under the Prevention of Terrorism legislation; corporal punishment; and restrictions upon adult homosexuals in Northern Ireland.

If it is accepted that a human rights measure is needed, the next question that needs consideration is its content. Most of those who support the introduction of a Bill of Rights point to the European Convention on Human Rights as a suitable model, but how valuable would this be?

Three matters in particular should be borne in mind. First the Convention is selective in the rights it seeks to protect, it contains no reference to a right to education, health care, or employment. It reflects a 'Western' view of individual rights, as opposed to a 'Socialistic' view. Secondly, the Convention includes many limitations upon the rights set forth, and does allow signatory states to derogate from some of its provisions in certain circumstances. For example the Convention does provide for freedom of association, but goes on to recognise that governments can limit this right if it is in the national interests to do so, thus the Civil Service Unions involved in the 'GCHQ' union ban dispute were not able to pursue their case under the Convention. Thirdly, a Bill of Rights can only be effective if it is protected to some extent from repeal or amendment by subsequent governments, and if subsequent legislation is applied only to the extent that it does not conflict with the Bill of Rights. To prevent changes being introduced by a subsequent Parliament would involve a major constitutional change in the nature of parliamentary sovereignty, with a marked increase in the powers of the judiciary. The controversy surrounding the status and effect of the European Communities Act 1972 provides an example of the difficulties that could be encountered. Many would feel that human rights are not in sufficient peril in the United Kingdom to justify such a constitutional upheaval.

* Debated on 6th February 1987; although it attracted 94 votes in support and only 16 in opposition, it was lost on the technical requirement that there had to be 100 MPs supporting the measure

14 PUBLIC ORDER

14.1 Introduction

Our enjoyment of basic human rights are not guaranteed by a constitutionally entrenched document. This constitutional position can be contrasted with other countries where such rights are defined in a single document. An example can be found in The Canada Charter. The UK is a signatory to the European Convention of Human Rights but it does not form part of our domestic law and, although influential in shaping policies in the UK, does not have legal force as such.

The consequence of the above position is that citizens in the UK can do as they wish as long as it is not against the law. Our freedoms are described as residual. There are many legal restrictions on our freedom to assemble and associate together. Such restrictions represent the political view of the extent to which a civil liberty should be restricted in the interests of social order and involves a balancing exercise which often results in emotive arguments between those who prioritise public order on the one hand and those who fear excessive state controls on the other.

Historically governments have reacted to threats to social order by introducing measures which are restrictive. Recent problems in Britain ranging from violence on football terraces to serious disorder in urban areas have resulted in the introduction of legislation which has increased police powers - the Police and Criminal Evidence Act 1984 - and recast the law relating to public order - the Public Order Act 1986. These two acts taken together are a significant step towards the codification of the law on public order but other significant measures coexist alongside them. It is therefore important to understand what restrictions exist to fully understand what freedoms we do in fact enjoy.

14.2 Key points

Common Law

a)   *Breach of the peace*

Section 40 of the Public Order Act 1986 specifically retains the common law powers to deal with or prevent a breach of the peace and s17(5) and (6) of the Police and Criminal Evidence Act preserve common law powers of entry to deal with breaches of the peace.

A precise definition of breach of the peace is difficult to give but it must involve an element of actual or apprehended violence to person or property. A police officer who has either witnessed a breach of the peace or who has reasonable grounds for believing that a breach of the peace is about to occur can arrest an offender without warrant. See: *R* v *Howell* [1982] QB 416; *R* v *Chief Constable of Devon and Cornwall ex parte CEGB* [1982] QB 458; *Moss* v *McLachlan* (1984) 149 JP 167.

b) *Entry into meetings*

While there is no doubt that the police have a right to be present in public places where there are fears of public disorder, there did exist some uncertainty as to their powers in respect of private premises where they had reason to believe a breach of the peace was imminent: See *Thomas* v *Sawkins* [1935] 2 KB 249.

Statutory Powers

c) *Obstruction of the police*

Under the Police Act 1964 any person who assaults the police in the execution of his duty or resists or wilfully obstructs the police in the course of his duty is guilty of an offence. Policing inevitably involves the exercise of discretion. In the context of public order the issue is the extent to which the police can lawfully intervene. See: *Duncan* v *Jones* [1936] 1 KB; *Piddington* v *Bates* [1960] 3 All ER 660.

d) *Obstruction of the highway*

Under the Highways Act 1980 a person is guilty of an offence if he wilfully obstructs the free passage of the highway. To initiate a meeting which results in such an obstruction can result in conviction even in circumstances where the highway was not completely blocked. See: *Arrowsmith* v *Jenkins* [1963] 2 QB 561; *Hirst and Agu* v *Chief Constable for West Yorkshire* [1987] Crim LR 330.

e) *Public Order Act 1986*

i) Public order offences

- The Public Order Act abolishes the common law offence of riot, rout, unlawful assembly and affray. It also abolishes the statutory offence of threatening behaviour under the Public Order Act 1936. These it replaces with an expanded range of public order offences - riot, violent disorder, affray, threatening behaviour and disorderly conduct.

- Section 1. The offence of riot is retained for the most serious public order offences.

  The difficult concept of common purpose and the execution of that common purpose is retained. This is to underline the seriousness of violent behaviour when committed collectively. Common purpose does not necessarily involve advance planning - a group of like minded individuals would probably be enough.

A person of reasonable firmness is not defined. Note that it is not necessary for this hypothetical person to be present.

A person must intend to use violence or be aware that his conduct may be violent. Violence is defined in s8.

The consent of the DPP is needed for a prosecution.

- Section 2. The offence of violent disorder is designed for application over a wide spectrum of situations ranging from major public disorder to minor group disturbances eg football hooliganism. It is a lesser offence than riot.

Note the similarities with riot - persons present together, the use or threat of unlawful violence, a person of reasonable firmness present at the scene being fearful for his safety.

However, the required number of persons is three, there is no requirement for a common purpose and the consent of the DPP is not necessary for a prosecution.

- Section 3. The new offence of affray penalises a person who uses or threatens violence towards another so as to cause a person of reasonable firmness to fear for his personal safety. Note that the requirements here are fairly straightforward. It seems that the offence anticipates the following sort of conduct - fighting outside pubs or football grounds and also on private premises. Threatening to fight would be included.

- Section 4. The Act abolishes s5 of the Public Order Act 1936 and replaces it with the offence in s4. The old s5 was used in a very wide variety of circumstances and in the 1984 miners strike some 4,000 miners were charged under that offence.

The concept of threatening, abusive or insulting words or behaviour is retained.

There must be an intention to provoke unlawful violence or a person must believe that unlawful violence will be used against him.

- Section 18 makes it an offence to use words or behaviour or display written material whereby racial hatred is likely to be stirred up.

There must be an intention to stir up racial hatred or having regard to all the circumstances it is likely to be stirred up.

- Section 19 deals with the publication or distribution of written material the consequence of which is racial hatred.

Note that the language of ss18 and 19 are similar to s4 and the same interpretive considerations will apply.

- Section 5 introduces a new offence. It is widely drawn and includes behaviour which would not have been previously considered a crime. It covers minor acts of hooliganism such as rowdy behaviour, banging on doors etc.

There is no need for the behaviour to cause or provoke violence. It need only be proved that harassment, alarm or distress are likely.

There are three specific defences: that the conduct was reasonable; that the defendant was inside a dwelling house and he had no reason to believe that a person outside would hear; the defendant had no reason to believe that there was any person within hearing or sight likely to be caused harassment, alarm or distress.

See: *Brutus* v *Cozens* [1973] AC 854; *Jordan* v *Burgoyne* [1963] 2 QB 744; *News Group Newspapers Ltd* v *Society of Graphic and Allied Trades* (1986) The Times 1 August; *Parkin* v *Norman* [1983] QB 92; *Mandla* v *Lee* [1983] 2 AC 548.

ii) Processions and demonstrations

- The Act lays down a more comprehensive legal framework for problems associated with processions and demonstrations. Additional powers are now given to the police to regulate static demonstrations and under s11 there is a requirement that notice of an intended march be given to the police.

- English law does not recognise a right to assemble although judges have commented that as a matter of public policy it is important that individuals should be able to protest. See Denning LJ in *Hubbard* v *Pitt* [1976] QB 142.

Section 16 defines public assembly as an assembly of 20 or more persons in a public place which is wholly or partly open to the air.

- Every procession or demonstration is inevitably an inconvenience to some and an obstruction to many and the discretionary enforcement of powers by the police is an important factor.

The police now must be informed by the organiser of a proposed march and the chief officer can impose conditions if he believes it may result in serious public disorder, serious damage to property or serious disruption to the life of the community: s12. A total ban can be imposed under s13 if the chief officer believes that his above powers are insufficient to prevent serious disorder resulting. The ban then applies to *all* processions.

Application is to the council and subject to the consent of the Home Secretary the ban will apply for a period not exceeding three months.

- Section 14 contains a new power for a senior police officer to impose conditions in relation to public assemblies but conditions may only govern the place, duration and number of persons present.

f) *Public Order Act 1936*

Section 1 of the Act makes it an offence to wear a uniform signifying membership of a political organisation. See *O'Moran* v *DPP* [1975] QB 364.

g) There are additional powers available to the state to suppress anti social behaviour which would be relevant in a public order context. The Police and Criminal Evidence Act 1984 gives the police certain powers of arrest for 'arrestable offences' which would include assault. The Prevention of Terrorism Act 1984 makes it an offence to belong to a proscribed organisation which includes of course the IRA.

14.3   Recent cases

Hirst and Agu v *Chief Constable for West Yorkshire* [1987] Crim LR 330

News Group Newspapers Ltd v *Society of Graphic and Allied Trades* (1986) The Times 1 August

14.4   Analysis of questions

Questions can be problem or essay. Included below are examples of each. A knowledge of the Public Order Act is essential and a methodical application of the provisions of the Act to any problem will earn marks. Whilst there have been many prosecutions under the Act in the Magistrates Court there have been few occasions when the higher courts have considered points of interpretation as yet. An essay question may require a broader if limited knowledge of the social background to the act's introduction.

14.5   Questions

QUESTION 1

What difference, if any, has the Public Order Act 1986 made to English law?

University of London LLB Examination
(for External Students) Constitutional Law June 1987 Q8

General comment

A relatively straightforward question concerning the new Public Order Act. Students should know the changes introduced by this Act and compare the new provisions with those existing at common law and under the Public Order Act 1936. A question increasingly less likely but the issues raised are relevant to other essay-type questions.

Skeleton solution

*   Introduction. General provisions of the Public Order Act 1986.

*   Abolition of common law riot, rout, unlawful assembly and affray. Introduction of statutory riot, violent disorder and affray.

*   Provisions relating to processions. Sections 12 and 13.

*   Provisions relating to assemblies. Section 14.

- Provisions relating to racial hatred.
- Causing fear or provocation of violence. Causing harassment, alarm or distress.
- Miscellaneous provisions.

Suggested solution

The Public Order Act 1986 was passed on 7 November 1986. Some provisions of the Act came into force on 1 January 1987. Most of the rest of the Act came into force on 1 April 1987. The Act firstly repeals certain provisions of the Public Order Act 1936. Secondly it abolishes the common law offences of riot, rout, unlawful assembly and affray. Third, it introduces new statutory offences to replace some of the common law offences abolished or statutory offences repealed. Fourth, it amends or repeals other statutory provisions including those concerning racial hatred. Fifth, it introduces new powers in relation to offences committed at or in connection with football matches. Sixth, it introduces miscellaneous provisions in relation to tampering with goods on sale and also mass trespass.

One of the main differences made to the law under the new Act is that the ancient common law offences of riot, rout, unlawful assembly and affray have been abolished and replaced by three statutory offences: riot, violent disorder and affray. The basis of these offences is no longer breach of the peace but fear for personal safety on the part of a person of reasonable firmness present at the scene.

As regards the Public Order Act 1936 this is largely repealed. Section 3 has been repealed and replaced by a new provision of greater scope and effect and has been extended to certain public assemblies. As was already the case under the old 1936 Act, s12 of the 1986 Act gives the police the power to impose conditions on certain processions and under s13 the chief officer of police may in certain circumstances prohibit processions in his district. The major difference under the new Act however is that now the organisers of public processions must give advance notice in writing to the police not less than six clear days before the date of any procession which is intended to demonstrate support for or opposition to the views or actions of any person or body of persons; or publicises a cause or campaign; or which marks or commemorates an event.

Another new development under the 1986 Act is contained in s14 which confers a new power allowing a senior police officer to impose conditions in relation to public assemblies. Under this section, if the senior police officer, having regard to the time or place at which and the circumstances in which any public assembly is being held or is intended to be held, reasonably believes that a) it may result in serious public disorder, serious damage to property or serious disruption to the life of the community, or b) the purpose of the persons organising it is the intimidation of others with a view to compelling them not to do an act they have a right to do, or to do an act they have a right not to do, he may give directions imposing on the persons organising or taking part in the assembly such conditions as to the place at which the assembly may be (or continue to be) held, its maximum duration, or the maximum number of persons who may constitute it, as appear to him necessary to prevent such disorder, damage, disruption or intimidation. However, there is still no power to ban an assembly. Section 16 defines 'public assembly' as an assembly of 20 or more persons in a public place which is wholly or partly open to the air.

Section 5A of the 1936 Act dealing with racial hatred has been restructured and amended to produce six new offences. Section 17 of the 1986 Act defines racial hatred as hatred against a group of persons in Great Britain defined by reference to colour, race, nationality (including citizenship) or ethnic or national origins. All six offences created by the Act require the consent of the Attorney-General to institute proceedings. All of these offences concern conduct which is threatening, abusive or insulting and which is intended or which is likely, having regard to all the circumstances, to stir up racial hatred. They are: i) using such words or behaviour or displaying such materials; ii) publishing or distributing such materials; iii) presenting or directing a public play which involves such words or behaviour; iv) distributing, showing or playing a recording of such visual images or sounds; v) certain participation in a broadcast or cable programme service which includes such images or sounds and; vi) possessing such material or recordings with a view to its being displayed, published, distributed, broadcast or included in a cable broadcast service.

Section 5 of the 1936 Act has also been repealed, and replaced by two new offences. Section 4 of the 1986 Act creates the offence of causing fear or provocation of violence. A person is guilty of an offence if he uses towards another person threatening, abusive or insulting words or behaviour, or distributes or displays to another person any writing, sign or other visible representation which is threatening, abusive or insulting, with intent to cause that person to believe that immediate unlawful violence will be used against him or another by any person, or to provoke the immediate use of unlawful violence by that person or another, or whereby that person is likely to believe that such violence will be used or it is likely that such violence will be provoked.

Section 5 of the 1986 Act creates the controversial offence of causing harassment, alarm or distress. A person is guilty of an offence if he uses threatening, abusive or insulting words or behaviour, or disorderly behaviour, or displays any writing, sign or other visible representation which is threatening, abusive or insulting, within the hearing or sight of a person likely to be caused harassment, alarm or distress thereby. Section 5 provides for three specific defences. First, that the defendant had no reason to believe that there was anyone within hearing or sight of his or her conduct who was likely to be harassed, alarmed or distressed; second, that he or she was inside a dwelling and had no reason to believe that the conduct would have been seen or heard by anyone outside; third, that his or her conduct was reasonable.

The 1986 Act also creates several miscellaneous offences. Under s30 a court by or before which a person is convicted or an offence connected with football may make an exclusion order prohibiting him from entering premises to attend a prescribed football match. Section 38 creates various offences connected with contamination of or interference with goods. Finally, s39 gives the most senior police officer present power to direct trespassers to leave land. The officer may arrest anyone who, knowing that such a direction has been given, fails to leave as soon as is reasonable practicable or, having left, re-enters within three months of the direction.

147

QUESTION 2

The PRO organisation arrange a procession through the streets of London. They do not ask anyone for permission. The ANTI organisation arrange a counter demonstration, again without seeking official permission. When the two marches converge on the Strand, violence breaks out. Nobody in the PRO march uses force except in self defence. A police constable orders the PRO marchers to stop their procession and to disperse. They continue to march and are arrested. Pleased with their success the ANTI marchers disperse and make their way home. A dozen of them decide to have some 'fun' on the Underground platform. They surround an old lady and begin to chant 'euthanasia, euthanasia'. She is alarmed by this and collapses. The ANTI marchers later discover that she was of an unusually weak disposition and had previously suffered heart attacks. But at the time they panic and run away. One of them is intent on escape and has no intent of causing further trouble. The others take the opportunity of lashing out violently at passers-by.

Which offences, if any, have been committed against the Public Order Act 1986?

Written by Editor March 1990

General comment

A question which demands a comprehensive knowledge of public order offences but a well prepared student should have no problem if application is logical and thorough. Clearly a good grasp of the Public Order Act 1986 is essential.

Skeleton solution

- Introduction. Effect of the 1986 Public Order Act.

- Powers of the police to impose conditions on possessions - s12. Common law powers to prevent a breach of peace.

- Section 1 Riot

  Section 2 Violent disorder

  Section 3 Affray

- Section 4

- Section 5

- Analyse and apply facts to above sections of the Act.

Suggested solution

The Public Order Act 1986 was passed on 7 November 1986. Some provisions of the Act came into force on 1 January 1987. Most of the rest of the Act came into force on 1 April 1987. The Act firstly repeals certain provisions of the Public Order Act 1936. Secondly, it abolishes the common law offences of riot, rout, unlawful assembly and affray. Third, it introduces new statutory offences to replace some of the common law offences abolished or statutory offences repealed. Fourth, it amends or repeals other statutory provisions including those concerning racial hatred. Fifth, it introduces new powers in relation to offences committed at or in connection with football matches. Sixth, it introduces miscellaneous provisions in relation to tampering with goods on sale and also mass trespass.

Regarding the problem for consideration, the PRO organisation have arranged a procession through the streets of London and have not asked for permission. While there is no requirement under the law that permission has to be obtained to hold a procession, under s11 of the Public Order Act 1986 the organisers of public processions must give advance notice in writing to the police not less than six clear days before the date of any procession which is intended to demonstrate support for or opposition to the views or actions of any person or body of persons; or publicise a cause or campaign; or which marks or commemorates an event. In not giving such notice the procession organisers therefore commit an offence. The same will be true of the organisers of the ANTI procession.

When the two groups converge violence, instigated by the ANTI marchers, breaks out and a police constable orders the PRO marchers to stop their procession and disperse. It is of course a fundamental principle of our law that one cannot be stopped from doing what one is lawfully entitled to do merely because others act unlawfully. However, s12 of the 1986 Act gives the police the power to impose conditions on certain processions if a senior police officer, having regard to the time or place at which and the circumstances in which, any public procession is being held or is intended to be held, reasonably believes that a) it may result in serious public disorder, serious damage to property or serious disruption to the life of the community, or b) the purpose of the persons organising it is the intimidation of others with a view to compelling them not to do an act they have a right to do, or to do an act they have a right not to do. Further, under s13 the chief officer of police may in certain circumstances prohibit processions in his district.

While the power therefore exists under the Public Order Act for the police to impose conditions on and even in some circumstances ban a lawful procession, it does not appear that the conditions for so doing apply in this particular case, and in any case they certainly may not be exercised by a mere constable. However, at common law a police officer has the power to take such steps as are reasonably necessary to prevent a breach of the peace and in so doing is acting in the execution of his duty so that a failure to obey would be an offence under s51(3) Police Act 1964 (*Duncan* v *Jones* (1936)) and if a breach of the peace is occurring or threatened there is a common law right to arrest preserved by the Police and Criminal Evidence Act 1984.

As regards the violence which takes place in the Strand and the actions of the ANTI marchers on the Underground platform, various offences under the Public Order Act 1986 may have been committed.

One of the main differences made to the law under the new Act is that the ancient common law offences of riot, rout, unlawful assembly and affray have been abolished and replaced by three statutory offences: riot, violent disorder and affray. The basis of these offences is no longer breach of the peace but fear for personal safety on the part of a person of reasonable firmness present at the scene. Section 1 redefines the offence of riot. Where 12 or more persons who are present together use or threaten unlawful violence and the conduct of them (taken together) is such as would cause a person of reasonable firmness present at the scene to fear for his personal safety, each of the persons using or threatening unlawful violence for the common purpose is guilty of violent disorder.

Section 3 redefines the offence of affray. A person is guilty of affray if he uses or threatens unlawful violence towards another and his conduct is such as would cause a person of reasonable firmness present at the scene to fear for his personal safety.

Section 5 of the 1936 Public Order Act has also been repealed, and replaced by two new offences. Section 4 of the 1986 Act creates the offence of causing fear or provocation of violence. A person is guilty of an offence if he uses towards another person threatening, abusive or insulting words or behaviour, or distributes or displays to another person any writing, sign or other visible representation which is threatening, abusive or insulting, with intent to cause that person to believe that immediate unlawful violence will be used against him or another by any person, or to provoke the immediate use of unlawful violence by that person or another, or whereby that person is likely to believe that such violence will be used or it is likely that such violence will be provoked.

Section 5 of the 1986 Act creates the controversial offence of causing harassment, alarm or distress. A person is guilty of an offence if he uses threatening, abusive or insulting words or behaviour, or disorderly behaviour, or displays any writing, sign or other visible representation which is threatening, abusive or insulting, within the hearing or sight of a person likely to be caused harassment, alarm or distress thereby. Section 5 provides for three specific defences. First, that the defendant had no reason to believe that there was anyone within hearing or sight of his or her conduct who was likely to be harassed, alarmed or distressed; second, that he or she was inside a dwelling and had no reason to believe that the conduct would have been seen or heard by anyone outside; third, that his or her conduct was reasonable.

From the facts given in the problem it appears that the actions of the ANTI organisation in the Strand could amount to riot, violent disorder and affray since it appears that the violence was instigated by them. However, the PRO organisation acting only in self defence do not seem to fall within the definitions of ss1 and 2 since they acted only in self defence, ie no *unlawful* violence.

When the ANTI demonstrators gather on the underground platform it seems they simply surround the old lady and chant 'euthanasia, euthanasia'. From the facts given it would seem doubtful whether it would be possible to establish 'use or threats of unlawful violence' so as to sustain charges under ss1, 2 and 3 and s4 also depends upon the threat of 'immediate unlawful violence'. It would therefore seem that the actions in respect of the old lady would have to be prosecuted under s5, causing harassment, alarm or distress. The words 'euthanasia, euthanasia' could be classified as threatening and since an old lady has been singled out for the treatment none of the defences seem appropriate. It will of course be no defence that the ANTI group was not aware of her unusually weak disposition. In *Jordan* v *Burgoyne* (1963), a case dealing with similar provisions in the old s5, Public Order Act 1936, it was made clear that the person using threatening, abusive or insulting words cannot look at their effect on a hypothetical reasonable audience but must take note of the effect on the actual audience addressed.

The ANTI demonstrators then disperse, one on his own, leaving 11 who commit acts of violence on passers by. Since there are then only 11 people no offence of riot can be established but violent disorder and affray charges are available, under ss2 and 3 of the 1986 Act respectively.

15 FREEDOM OF EXPRESSION

15.1 Introduction

15.2 Key points

15.3 Recent cases and statutes

15.4 Question analysis

15.5 Question

15.1 Introduction

English law relies on the principle that what is not prohibited is permitted and attempts are made to achieve a balance between one individual's right to express his opinions, another's right to be protected from the worst excesses of those views and the state's interest in ensuring that expressed opinions do not undermine either public order or state security. The result is a wide range of specific offences to provide remedies to either individuals or the state when views expressed go beyond what is considered tolerable. The area includes such diverse topics as theatre censorship and state security, contempt of court, obscene publications and the right to privacy.

While individual syllabuses may emphasise different facets of freedom of expression, the issue in each case is generally whether a balance between competing interests has been achieved.

15.2 Key points

a) *The protection of the State*

 i) Sedition

   This common law offence is now largely of historical interest as other offences have largely superseded the need to prosecute for sedition.

   More recently the element of incitement to violence has been stressed. *R v Caunt* (1948) unreported.

 ii) Incitement to disaffection

   It is an offence to undermine the loyalty of:

   • a police officer: s53 Police Act 1964; or

   • a member of the armed forces: Incitement to Disaffection Act 1934. See *R v Arrowsmith* [1975] QB 678.

 iii) Incitement to racial hatred

   • Threats, abuse and insults which are likely to result in unlawful violence are criminal: Public Order Act 1986 s4.

- Threats, abuse or insults which are intended or are likely to stir up racial hatred are specifically dealt with by ss17-23 Public Order Act 1986. The offences are unlikely to be committed by those who use reasoned argument: *Jordan* v *Burgoyne* [1963] 2 QB 744.

Note the meaning of racial group - a group of persons defined by reference to colour, race, nationality or ethnic or national origins: *Mandla* v *Dowell Lee* [1983] 2 AC 548.

iv) Blasphemy

- Blasphemy is a common law offence committed through attacks on the Christian religion or the existence of God.

The Law Commission has recommended that the offence be abolished and that any statutory alternative not be restricted to attacks upon Christianity.

- In *R* v *Lemon* [1979] AC 617 it was held that there was no need for an intention to blaspheme, publication was enough. Publication need not necessarily lead to a breach of the peace.

v) Criminal libel

Criminal libel covers cases of libel where there is considered to be some threat to the preservation of the peace. Prosecutions are rare and only with the order of a High Court judge: *Goldsmith* v *Pressdram Ltd* [1976] 3 WLR 191.

vi) Freedom of communication and information

- Government has a duty to preserve the security of the State. National security includes not only measures intended to protect the State from espionage but also all matters that are considered subversive. Governments are often seen as using the cloak of national security to prevent the communication of information motivated by the objective of secrecy.

- Official Secrets Acts

Section 1 of the Official Secrets Act 1911 creates offences of espionage. It is not restricted to spying but includes acts of sabotage: *Chandler* v *DPP* [1964] AC 763.

Section 2 created some 2000 offences directed at the misuse of information. It was criticised for being used to keep policy making free of outside scrutiny.

In 1989 section 2 was repealed by the Official Secrets Act 1989. This legislation criminalises the communication of information about security and intelligence matters. There is no possibility of acquittal on the grounds that the publication was in the public interest. In addition there are offences to punish the disclosure of information about defence, foreign policy, police operations and relations with other countries if such disclosure is likely to be damaging.

153

- **'D' Notices**

  A form of extra legal censorship which depends on co-operation between governments and the press with the objective of achieving a ban on the publication of matters which are considered likely to jeopardise national security.

- **Interception of Communications Act 1985**

  Under the Act it is an offence to intercept communications (specifically telephone communications) unless authorised by the Secretary of State who may issue a warrant in the interests of national security or for the purpose of preventing serious crime or for the purpose of safeguarding the economic well being of the United Kingdom. See generally *Malone v UK* (1985) 7 EHRR 14.

- **Breach of confidence**

  An equitable doctrine to ensure that a person should not take unfair advantage of confidences obtained: *Argyll v Argyll* [1967] Ch 302.

  It is worth noting in this context because of the attempt made by the government in the 'Spycatcher' affair to assert that members of the security services owe a lifelong duty of confidentiality to the Crown: *Attorney-General v Guardian Newspapers Ltd, The Observer Ltd, Times Newspapers Ltd* [1988] 3 All ER 545.

b) *Obscene publications*

i) The trade in pornography is lucrative and the State seeks to limit publication to limit 'depravity'. There are statutory and common law offences.

ii) Obscene Publications Act 1959

An obscene article is one where the effect '... if taken as a whole, would tend to deprave and corrupt persons who are likely having regard to all the circumstances to read, see or hear the matter contained or embodied in it': s1.

- Article is defined widely and includes pictures, books and film negatives.

- The definition of obscene requires the jury to consider whether the article has a tendency to deprave and corrupt and this has caused inconsistency. It is not limited to sexual matters: *John Calder (Publishers) v Powell* [1965] 1 QB 509; *DPP v A and BC Chewing Gum Ltd* [1968] 1 QB 159.

- Policing the trade in pornography is difficult - 'an attempt to eradicate the ineradicable' (Robert Mark, ex Chief Commissioner for the Metropolis, in *Policing a Perplexed Society* (1977)). See *R v Metropolitan Police Commissioner ex parte Blackburn* [1973] QB 241.

- Section 3 confers search, seizure and forfeiture powers.

- Section 4 makes it a defence if the material is 'for the public good on the grounds that it is in the interests of science, literature, art or learning ...'.

Whether publication is for the public good is for the jury to decide.

iii) The Obscene Publications Act 1964 allows the police to seize material if the material was 'in possession for gain' thus it can be effective - material can be seized - before publication.

iv) Other legislation

This includes Customs Consolidation Act 1876, the Children and Young Persons (Harmful Publications) Act 1955 and the Post Office Act 1953.

v) Common law offences

- Conspiracy to corrupt public morals: *Shaw* v *DPP* [1962] AC 220.

- Conspiracy to outrage public decency: *Knuller* v *DPP* [1973] AC 435.

c) *Contempt of court*

i) Civil contempts

The breach of or disobedience to an order of the court: *Harman* v *Home Secretary* [1982] 2 WLR 338.

ii) Criminal contempts

The objective here is to ensure both the fairness of a trial and also that the judiciary is accorded respect.

iii) Contempt of Court Act 1981

The Act clarified the position regarding newspaper publication of matters of public interest which could prejudice the outcome of court proceedings by the following reforms.

See also *Attorney-General* v *Times Newspapers* [1974] AC 273, a case which went to the European Court of Human Rights.

- It is an offence 'to interfere with the course of justice in particular legal proceedings regardless of intent' where the proceedings in question are active: s1.

- There is no offence if there was no reason to suspect that proceedings are active (s3) or that publication is a discussion in good faith of public affairs: *Attorney-General* v *English* [1982] 2 WLR 278.

- Section 10 gives limited protection to journalists of their sources unless disclosure is necessary in the interests of justice, national security or for the prevention of disorder or crime: *Secretary of State for Defence* v *Guardian Newspapers Ltd* [1984] 2 WLR 268.

d) *Censorship*

i) Theatres are subject to the laws on obscenity, defamation and incitement to racial hatred.

ii) Cinemas are licensed by the local authority which attaches conditions and recommendations of the British Board of Film Censors are usually followed.

iii) Broadcasting

Both the BBC and IBA are under a duty to provide programmes which comply with good taste and decency and to preserve political impartiality. This last point has sometimes caused political controversy with governments.

e) *Defamation*

i) Publication of material which 'tends to lower a person in the estimation of right thinking members of society generally' (Lord Atkin in *Sim* v *Stretch* (1936) 52 TLR 669) is a tort and gives rise to a civil action for damages.

ii) Note the defences available.

f) *Prior restraint*

A person whose interests are likely to be affected by the publication of material or the Attorney-General in his role as guardian of the public interest can apply to the court for an injunction restraining such publication. The injunction is interim until such time as a full hearing of the issues can take place: see *Attorney-General* v *Guardian Newspapers* [1987] 3 All ER 316; *Attorney-General* v *Newspaper Publishing plc* [1987] 3 All ER 276.

15.3 Recent cases and statutes

Official Secrets Act 1989

Interception of Communications Act 1985

Attorney-General v *Guardian Newspapers Ltd, The Observer Ltd, Times Newspapers Ltd* [1988] 3 All ER 545

15.4 Question analysis

London University has not questioned students directly on this topic in recent years. Other examiners may emphasise a particular area, for example State security, with a view to examining students' knowledge on that specific subject. The topic does lend itself to a general essay type question eg 'consider to what extent in your view a balance has been achieved between competing interests in the areas of ...' and an examiner could then identify the areas the student should focus on.

In any case a general knowledge of the topic is important in, for example, answering a question on a Bill of Rights.

15.5 Question

To what extent does the law successfully balance competing interests in the area of press freedom?

Written by Editor May 1990

Skeleton solution

*   Introduction - nature of freedom of speech in the United Kingdom - remedies available.

*   Prior restraint - an evaluation of the effect of prior restraint on the media.

*   Breach of confidence - its use particularly by government.

*   Official Secrets Act 1989.

*   Contempt of court.

*   The individual and the press - remedies and contrasts with the above.

Suggested solution

Freedom of speech is fundamental to a free society. It is protected by Article 10 of the European Convention on Human Rights but of course the convention is not directly applicable in UK courts. The position in the United Kingdom is that individual members of the state are free to express views and opinions that are not against the numerous laws that restrict freedom of speech and to this extent the law attempts to balance competing rights. The press has a fundamental role to perform in informing the public, not least on government activities. However, individuals have a right not to be offended or abused and the state has a right to prevent the publication of sensitive material that could, for example, jeopardise national security. There is an inherent conflict here and some of the ways in which the law deals with that conflict in relation to press freedom will now be examined.

The major restrictions on press freedom are to be found in the laws on defamation, breach of confidence and contempt of court.

It is important at the outset to draw a distinction between prior restraint and subsequent penalties. Blackstone (in his *Commentaries* (1765)) emphasised the importance in a free society of laying no prior restraints on publications - 'every free man has an undoubted right to lay what sentiments he pleases before the public; to forbid this is to destroy the freedom of the press ...' - and his sentiments were included in the first amendment to the American Constitution. It is arguable that prior restraint has become relatively easy to obtain in Britain either by the person whose interests are affected or by the Attorney-General as 'guardian of the public interest'. The injunction is interim and the applicant has to show that he has an arguable case, that the balance of convenience is against publishing and damages are not an adequate remedy. That balance of convenience is normally in favour of a ban and some writers (see G. Robertson, *Freedom, the Individual and the Law*) argue that this can amount to political interference with free speech. In *Attorney-General* v *BBC* (1987) the government was successful in getting an interim injunction against a series entitled 'My Country Right or Wrong' on the grounds that ex-employees of the security services might have breached confidences during interviews.

Injunctions can also be granted to protect commercial interests when the courts balance the public's right to information against the private interest in ensuring that discussion should be prevented. In this context the private interest will be to protect trade secrets whilst the public interest may relate to the effect for example of a drug: *Schering Chemicals* v *Falkman Ltd* (1981). An injunction once granted binds third parties: *Attorney-General* v *Observer Newspapers Ltd* (1988). Whilst the nature of the injunction is limited to the period until trial, it may well be that the information may by then be no longer important.

Breach of confidence is a civil matter providing protection where information is given in circumstances of confidence. It can include intimate communications between husband and wife (*Duke of Argyll* v *Duchess of Argyll* (1967)), trade secrets (*Lion Laboratories* v *Evans* (1984)) and often arises from a contract of employment. Claims to confidentiality can be defeated if the claimed confidences relate to criminal activity or if the disclosure serves the public interest. A confidence ceases to be a confidence once it is in the public domain. In *Attorney-General* v *Guardian Newspapers and others* (1988) the House of Lords held that given a government secret was in the public domain - in this case the information was obtainable in Australia and the USA - then the remedy should not be available to prevent British citizens reading it. Nevertheless, the court confirmed the lifelong duty of confidentiality owed by members of the security services. The public interest may continue to be served, however, where the revelations contain substantial allegations of wrongdoing.

Governments are concerned to limit information which is of a sensitive nature in terms of national security but also may be inclined to prevent publication where information is simply politically embarrassing. The use of the discredited s2 of the Official Secrets Act 1911 provides evidence of the preoccupation of governments with secrecy. In *R* v *Aitken* (1974) the government prosecuted under s2 for the publication of information already in the public domain and in the celebrated case of *R* v *Ponting* (1985) the jury found not guilty a civil servant who had 'leaked' information to an opposition MP which revealed that the government was attempting to deceive Parliament. Section 2 of the Act has been repealed by the Official Secrets Act 1989. Journalists and editors can be imprisoned if they encourage civil servants to make disclosures or publish such disclosures. During the debate, attention focused on whether there should be a 'public interest' defence, but amendments to the Bill were successfully resisted. Under s5 members of the press can be successfully prosecuted if they publish information which they know is protected by the Act and they had reason to believe the publication would be damaging to the interests of the United Kingdom. If information is published from former or serving members of the security service the offence is one of strict liability. It is notable that the court in *Attorney-General* v *Guardian Newspapers and others* (1988) accepted the principle of a public interest defence in breach of confidence actions which the government was anxious not to see in the Official Secrets Act 1989.

It is essential that court proceedings are not disrupted and justice is not impeded through press comment on cases in progress. In *Attorney-General* v *News Group Newspapers Ltd* (1987) an injunction to restrain further publication of allegedly defamatory material was refused because the trial was some months away and a substantial risk to proceedings would not result. Clearly if the press were to publish details of a person's previous convictions shortly before trial or publish a picture of someone involved in identification evidence there would be contempt. The Contempt of Court Act 1981 - legislation which followed the decision of the European Court of Human Rights involving the Sunday Times - limits contempt. There must be a substantial risk to proceedings - s2 and under s5 a discussion in the media in good faith where the risk to legal proceedings is incidental to the proceedings. This situation arose in *Attorney-General* v *English* (1983) where the discussion in the press fell under the protection of s5. Section 10 of the Act provides for the protection of journalistic sources unless 'it be established to the satisfaction of the court that disclosure is necessary in the interests of justice or national security or for the prevention of disorder or crime.' The courts have tended to order disclosure however eg *Secretary of State for Defence* v *Guardian Newspapers Ltd* (1984) and very recently in *X Ltd* v *Morgan Grampian Ltd and Others* (1990).

While there are many remedies available to the government to restrict press freedom, the protections available to individuals are more limited. The action of defamation can be brought but the expense involved is often prohibitive. The private interests of individuals and the lack of a comprehensive law on privacy in this country all too often leave the individual with no remedy: *Re X (a minor)* (1975). The Press Council considers complaints against newspapers but in practice has little effect against newspapers which invade privacy in the interests of sensationalism.

16 POLICE POWERS

16.1 Introduction

16.2 Key points

16.3 Recent cases

16.4 Analysis of questions

16.5 Question

16.1 Introduction

This is an important constitutional law topic covering as it does the powers of the police to stop and search an individual on the street and enter his premises. Despite its importance some examination boards notably University of London LLD External have only rarely set a question on this particular area of civil liberties. You should check your particular examination syllabus and past papers to establish whether this is a likely examination topic in your case.

16.2 Key points

Virtually all police powers are now contained in the Police and Criminal Evidence Act 1984 - commonly referred to as PACE - and the codes of practice accompanying the Act.

You must know the following key sections of the 1984 Act.

a)   *Sections 1-3*

These are the stop and search provisions.

They allow an officer to stop and search individuals and vehicles provided:

i)   they are in public places and

ii) the officer has reasonable grounds to suspect that he will find articles relating to:

- burglary
- theft
- joy riding
- obtaining property by deception

or that he will find an offensive weapon.

Remember that apart from sections 1-3 the power to search is limited to those who have been arrested *and* are at a police station: s32.

b) *Sections 17-18*

These provisions allow an officer to enter and search premises *without* a warrant. But note the limitations.

He may only do so in order:

i) to arrest and/or

ii) to search the premises of an already arrested person for evidence relating to the offence for which they person was arrested or any other 'arrestable' offence.

Remember the definitions of an arrestable offence - generally one that carries a maximum penalty in excess of five years eg theft, burglary: s24.

c) *Section 19*

This section gives a general right of seizure provided an officer is *lawfully* on the premises ie:

i) he has a search warrant; or

ii) he has entered pursuant to s17.

d) *Section 24*

This section gives power to arrest anyone without a warrant provided it is an 'arrestable offence' as defined above.

e) *Section 56*

This section allows anyone who has been arrested and is at a police station the right to inform someone of his arrest as soon as is reasonably practicable.

f) *Section 58*

This gives an arrested person held in custody the right to consult a solicitor privately at any time.

This is an extremely important provision - in particular a person has a right by reason of this section to have his solicitor present before he is interviewed in relation to the offence for which he has been arrested.

g) *Section 76*

This is a most important evidential provision allowing a 'confession' to be given in evidence against an accused even though technically it would be hearsay evidence ie a statement made outside court by a person other than the one giving evidence and put forward to show the truth of what has been said.

Note the wide definition of a confession namely any statement wholly or partly adverse to the maker: s82.

Section 76, however, guards against the risk of confessions brought about by oppression by putting the onus of proof on the prosecution to show that it was not obtained by either:

i) oppression; or

ii) anything done or said which might render it unreliable.

Unless the prosecution can show this, the confession will not be admissable.

h) *Section 78*

This section goes hand in hand with s76 but is much wider because it applies to *any* evidence - not simply confessions.

It gives the court a discretion to exclude any evidence which, having regard to the circumstances in which it was obtained, would have such an adverse influence on the fairness of the proceedings that the court ought not to admit it.

This section is aimed at giving a court a discretion to exclude evidence obtained in breach of PACE eg an illegal search under s17 or an interview where access to a solicitor under s56 was denied.

A confession may not be excluded under s76 but may nevertheless be excluded under s78: *R v Mason* [1988] 1 WLR 139.

Furthermore, breaches of the Codes of Guidance (see following section) may also lead to exclusion of evidence under s78.

i) *The Codes of Guidance*

The major code provisions are:

i) once persons are suspected of a crime they should be cautioned;

ii) basic comforts such as breaks for refreshment, proper rest, adequate heating and ventilation should be afforded whilst a person is in custody and being interviewed;

iii) consent to an identification parade is required. If a person is suspected it is wrong to show a witness photographs before asking that witness to pick someone out at an identification parade;

iv) if photographs are sown to a witness a minimum of 12 photographs ought to be shown.

16.3   Recent cases

R v Mason [1988] 1 WLR 139

R v Fulling [1987] 2 All ER 65

R v Samuel [1988] 2 All ER 135

16.4 Analysis of questions

As mentioned in the introduction (16.1), no questions on police powers have been set in recent years by some examination boards (including the University of London LLB External).

If this area is examined the likely examination question will be a problem solving exercise setting out a series of police actions eg entering premises, searching, seizing evidence, arresting an individual, and asking the candidate to comment on the legality or otherwise of the police actions.

16.5 Question

PC Black was called to the premises of Smiths (Jewellers) Limited following a report of a theft. When he arrived the owner, James Smith, told him that £450 had been stolen from his safe. There had been no sign of any break in or any damage to the safe itself. Smith told PC Black that he suspected an 'inside job' and named Terry Jones as a likely suspect. Terry Jones had only been employed by Smith for a few weeks and he knew the safe's combination.

PC Black went around to Terry Jones's house intending to arrest him. When he arrived no-one was in but the back door was not locked and PC Black entered the premises. Having established that Terry was not in PC Black proceeded to search the house and in an upstairs wardrobe he found £400 in cash wrapped in a pullover.

Just as he finished his search Terry Jones entered the house. PC Black asked Terry where he had been and whether he knew anything about the break in at Smiths Jewellers. Terry replied that he knew nothing about the theft. He was then searched by PC Black who found another £50 in cash in Terry's jacket pocket. Terry was asked where he got the money from and replied that it had 'nothing to do with' PC Black.

PC Black then arrested Terry and cautioned him. He took him to the police station where he was charged by the custody sergeant with theft.

PC Black then placed Terry in an interview room and asked him to make a statement. Terry asked whether he could speak to his solicitor before he answered any question but was told that was impossible. Terry refused to answer any questions and was kept in the interview room for a further six hours without being given any refreshments or being allowed to use the toilet.

Nevertheless, Terry still refused to answer any questions. However PC Black then told Terry that they were going to arrest and charge his eight months pregnant wife with receiving stolen money. However Terry was told that if he 'held his hands up' to the crime the police would not involve his wife.

Thereupon Terry signed a statement confessing to the theft.

Discuss the validity of PC Black's actions in this matter.

Written by Editor March 1990

163

Skeleton solution

- Was the entry lawful? Yes, because he had reason to believe Terry was guilty of an arrestable offence and might be at his house.

- Was the search legal? No, because he had no search warrant and had not arrested Terry when he searched the wardrobe.

- Was the search of Terry legal? No, because he had not been arrested when he was searched and it was not a public place therefore ss1-3 PACE not applicable.

- Was the initial questioning of Terry proper? No, because he suspected him immediately yet did not caution Terry before asking him any questions in breach of the Code of Guidance.

- The interview - in breach of Code of Guidance in way interview conducted. Wrong to deny access to solicitor: s58 PACE.

- The confession - oppressive/unreliable within meaning of s76 - *R* v *Fulling* (1987), *R* v *Samuel* (1988).

- Would evidence be admissible? Even though evidence obtained illegally court has discretion to allow its admissability. However strong argument that such illegally obtained evidence would be excluded because of s78.

Suggested solution

This question demands a discussion of police powers and in particular, the limitations on such power laid down by the provisions of the Police and Criminal Evidence Act 1984 (PACE).

When PC Black went to Terry's house he did so with the intention of arresting him for the theft at the jewellers. Accordingly he had a right to enter the premises in order to arrest Terry - theft is an arrestable offence and Black had reason to believe that Terry would be at home: s17 PACE.

However Black did not have a search warrant. Whilst s18 of PACE allows the search of premises of an arrested person, when the wardrobe was searched Terry had not yet been arrested. The finding of the £400 was as a result of an illegal search; this may well lead a court to exclude evidence of this find pursuant to s78 PACE, a matter I return to later.

Furthermore, the search of Terry was illegal. He had not been arrested when he was searched and he was searched inside his house, that is to say a private place. The power to stop and search only applies to public places (see ss1-3 PACE).

Since Black suspected Terry immediately the Code of Guidance required that he caution Terry before asking him any questions. Accordingly evidence of Terry's refusal to give an explanation as to where he got the £50 from may, once again, be excluded under s78 PACE.

The interview at the station can be attacked on a number of grounds. Firstly s58 PACE gives a right to have a solicitor present on request of an accused. Black's refusal to allow access to a solicitor was a clear breach of s58.

Secondly in making Terry remain in the interview room for such a lengthy period without refreshment or being permitted to use the toilet, Black was in breach of the Code of Guidance.

The above two reasons would make any statement made by Terry liable to be excluded by reason of s78 in any event.

However, the confession is very likely to be excluded by reason of s76 PACE. Whilst this section allows a confession to be admitted in evidence it will not be allowed in unless the prosecution can prove that it was not made by reason of oppression or something said or done to make it unreliable.

Terry would argue that the way he was treated in the interview room amounted to oppression and, in any event, the threat about charging his wife was something said to make the confession unreliable. In *R* v *Fulling* (1987) Lord Lane included 'cruel treatment' under the heading of oppression. The treatment of Terry during the interview does appear to be 'cruel'. Furthermore in *R* v *Samuel* (1988) the refusal of access to a solicitor was deemed to be a matter making a confession unreliable.

It is most probable, therefore, that the confession would be excluded by reason of s76 but, in any event, it may well be excluded under s78. In *R* v *Mason* (1988) it was held that confessions could be caught by both s76 and s78.

I have referred to s78 a great deal in this answer. It provides that unfairly obtained evidence may be excluded at the discretion of the court. The point to note here, therefore, is that while much of the evidence against Terry has been illegally obtained the court still has a discretion to admit it. However, equally it can exclude it under s78 which permits exclusion if it appears that, having regard to the way the evidence was obtained, its admission in evidence would have an adverse effect on the fairness of the trial. The tendency of courts is to use s78 in favour of defendants rather than against them ie evidence is normally excluded.

In summary, therefore, most of the evidence against Terry is likely to be excluded and Terry will probably not be convicted of this crime. The finding of the money was pursuant to illegal searches and is likely to be excluded under s78. The confession will be excluded under either s76 or s78.

HLT GROUP PUBLICATIONS FOR THE LLB EXAMINATIONS

Our publications, written by specialists, are used widely by students at universities, polytechnics and colleges throughout the United Kingdom and overseas.

Textbooks
These are designed as working books to provide students with a valuable framework on which to base their studies. They are updated each year to reflect new developments and changing trends.

Casebooks
These are designed as companion volumes to the Textbooks and incorporate important cases, statutes as appropriate, and other material, together with detailed commentaries.

Revision WorkBooks
For first degree law students, these provide questions and answers for all topics in each law subject. Every topic has sections on key points, recent cases and statutes, further reading etc.

Suggested Solutions
These are available to past London University LLB examination papers and provide the student with an invaluable revision aid and an insight into the techniques essential to examination success.

The books listed below can be ordered through your local bookshops or obtained direct from the publisher using this order form. Telephone, Fax or Telex orders will also be accepted. Quote your Access or Visa card numbers for priority orders. To order direct from the publisher please enter the cost of the titles you require, fill in the despatch details and send it with your remittance to the HLT Group Ltd.

ORDER FORM

LLB PUBLICATIONS	Textbooks		Casebooks		Revision WorkBooks		Sug. Sol. 1984/88		Sug. Sol. 1989	
	Cost £	£	Cost £	£	Cost £	£	Cost £	£	Cost £	£
L01 Criminal Law	12.95		16.95		9.95		14.95		3.95	
L02 Constitutional Law	12.95		16.95		9.95		14.95		3.95	
L03 English Legal System	12.95		14.95				*6.95		3.95	
L04 Law of Contract	12.95		15.95		9.95		14.95		3.95	
L05 Law of Tort	12.95		16.95				14.95		3.95	
L06 Law of Trusts	12.95		16.95		9.95		14.95		3.95	
L07 Land Law	12.95		18.95		9.95		14.95		3.95	
L08 Jurisprudence	14.95				9.95		14.95		3.95	
L09 Administrative Law	15.95		18.95				14.95		3.95	
L10 Law of Evidence	17.95		14.95		9.95		14.95		3.95	
L11 Commercial Law	17.95		18.95		9.95		14.95		3.95	
L13 Pub. Int. Law	16.95		14.95		9.95		14.95		3.95	
L14 Succession	14.95		15.95		9.95		14.95		3.95	
L16 Family Law	14.95		18.95				14.95		3.95	
L17 Company Law	16.95		18.95		9.95		14.95		3.95	
L18 Revenue Law	14.95		18.95		9.95		14.95		3.95	
L20 European Community Law	15.95									

Cut along dashed line   * 1987 and 1988 only

DETAILS FOR DESPATCH OF PUBLICATIONS
Please insert your full name below

Please insert below the style in which you would like correspondence to be addressed to you
TITLE Mr, Miss etc.   INITIALS   SURNAME/FAMILY NAME

Address to which study material is to be sent (please ensure someone will be present to accept delivery of your College Publications.)

POSTAGE & PACKING
You are welcome to purchase study material from the College at 200 Greyhound Road W14 9RY, during normal working hours.

If you wish to order by post this may be done direct from the College. Postal charges are as follows.

UK   -   all orders over £25 - no charge; orders below £25 - £1.50.
OVERSEAS -   all orders are sent by airmail and the charge is £6 for the first item, an additional £4 for the second item and an additional £3 for the third and for every additional item. If ordering *Suggested Solutions 1989 only* add 30% to the charge for the Suggested Solutions ordered.

The College cannot accept responsibility in respect of postal delays or losses in the postal systems.

DESPATCH All cheques must be cleared before material is despatched.

SUMMARY OF ORDER

Date of order: /   /

Cost of publications ordered: £
Add: Postage and packing United Kingdom (see above)   £
Overseas Air Mail: First item at £6; Second item at £4;
 Additional items at £3; Suggested Solutions only: 30%

Total cost of order: £

Please ensure that you enclose a cheque or draft payable to The HLT Group Ltd for the above amount, or charge to ☐ Access ☐ Visa

Card Number

Expiry Date   /   /   Signature _____

Your completed form and remittance should be sent to :
The HLT Group Ltd, Despatch Department, 200 Greyhound Road, London W14 9RY.
Telephone: (01) 385 3377 Telex: 266386 Fax: (01) 381 3377.